W9-ALX-043

READING/WRITING COMPANION

Mc
Graw
Hill
Education

COVER: Nathan Love, Erwin Madrid

mheducation.com/prek-12

Copyright © McGraw-Hill Education

All rights reserved. No part of this publication may be
reproduced or distributed in any form or by any means,
or stored in a database or retrieval system, without the
prior written consent of McGraw-Hill Education,
including, but not limited to, network storage or
transmission, or broadcast for distance learning.

Send all inquiries to:
McGraw-Hill Education
Two Penn Plaza
New York, NY 10121

ISBN: 978-0-07-901832-8
MHID: 0-07-901832-7

Printed in the United States of America.

4 5 6 7 8 9 LMN 23 22 21 20   B

Welcome to Wonders!

Read exciting **Literature**, **Science**, and **Social Studies** texts!

★ **LEARN** about the world around you!

★ **THINK**, **SPEAK**, and **WRITE** about genres!

★ **COLLABORATE** in discussion and inquiry!

★ **EXPRESS** yourself!

my.mheducation.com

Use your student login to read core texts, practice grammar and spelling, explore research projects and more!

(t) azaharphotography/iStock/Getty Images; (cl) Michael Svoboda/Getty Images; (cr) Don Paulson Photography/Purestock/SuperStock; (bl) ziggy_mars/Shutterstock.com; (bc) VaLiza/Shutterstock.com; (br) vipman/Shutterstock.com

UNIT 5

GENRE STUDY 1 **EXPOSITORY TEXT**

GENRE STUDY 2 **REALISTIC FICTION**

GENRE STUDY 3 EXPOSITORY TEXT

WRAP UP THE UNIT

Digital Tools Find this eBook and other resources at **my.mheducation.com**

Ed George/National Geographic/Getty Images

GENRE STUDY 1 NARRATIVE NONFICTION

GENRE STUDY 2 HISTORICAL FICTION

Echo/Cultura/Getty Images

GENRE STUDY **3 POETRY**

WRAP UP THE UNIT

 Digital Tools Find this eBook and other resources at **my.mheducation.com**

Talk About It

When you look at a peacock feather, you see rings of color. But if you look at that same feather under a microscope, suddenly it resembles a pinecone. What would you like to examine under a microscope?

Write words in the web that describe details of the peacock you see in the photograph. Next, look at an object in your classroom from far away and then up close. Describe to a partner what you see.

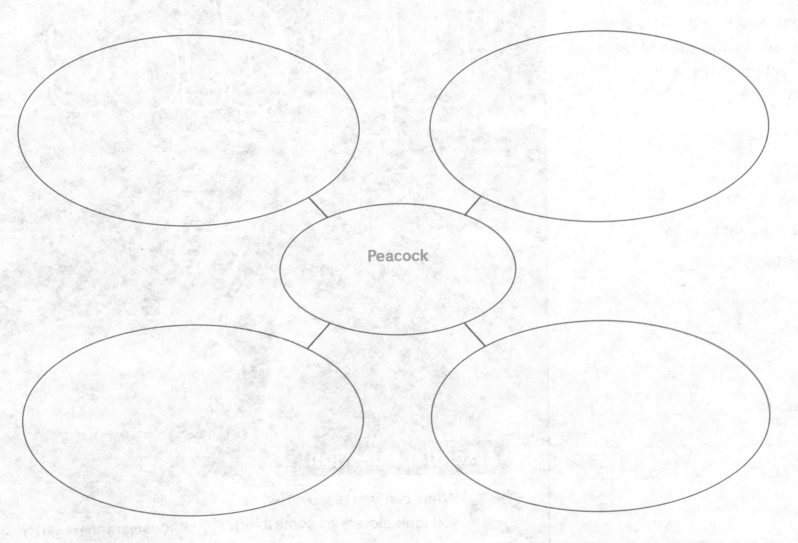

Peacock

Go online to **my.mheducation.com** and read the "How Old Is Your Water?" blast. Think about the water you drank today. What stages of the water cycle did the water travel through? Blast back your response.

Don Paulson Photography/Purestock/SuperStock

TAKE NOTES

Previewing a text helps you learn more about what you will be reading. Read the title and captions, and look at the images. Then predict what you will learn in this selection. Write your prediction here.

_____

_____

_____

As you read, make note of:

Interesting Words _____

_____

_____

_____

Key Details _____

_____

_____

_____

_____

_____

Your World Up Close

Essential Question

? What can you discover when you look closely at something?

Read about a tool that allows us to see everyday objects up close.

Compare these gritty grains of sugar with the magnified sugar crystal in the background.

(t) Zoonar RF/Getty Images; (b) koosen/iStock/Getty Images

Does the picture on the left show a diamond or a glass prism? Look closer. Take a step back. You are *too* close.

It is a picture of a sugar crystal. This extreme close-up was taken by an electron microscope, a tool that can **magnify** an item to thousands of times its actual size.

Pictures taken with a high-tech electron microscope are called photomicrographs. The sugar crystal on the left may look huge, but the word *micro* means small. We are seeing a small part of the sugar crystal up close.

Photomicrography dates back to 1840, when a scientist named Alfred Donné first photographed images through a microscope. Around 1852, a German pharmacist made the first version of a camera that took photomicrographs. In 1882, Wilson "Snowflake" Bentley of Vermont became the first person to use a camera with a built-in **microscope** to take pictures of snowflakes. His photographs showed that there is no such thing as a **typical** snowflake. Each is unique. Nowadays, we have electron micrographs.

These electron micrographs show that snowflakes are shaped like hexagons.

(r, c, l) Marion Owen/Design Pics/Getty Images

FIND TEXT EVIDENCE

Read

Paragraphs 1-3

Summarize

Circle key details you would use to summarize the most important ideas about electron microscopes.

Paragraph 4

Sequence

Underline the event that came next after Alfred Donné took images through a microscope. Who took the first photomicrographs of snowflakes?

_____

_____

Reread

Author's Craft

How does the author use photographs and captions to support and add to the information in the text?

FIND TEXT EVIDENCE

Read

Paragraphs 1–3

Summarize

Circle details you would use to summarize what electron microscopes helped scientists see that they never saw before.

Sequence

Draw a box around the phrase in paragraph 3 that shows the author is using a sequence text structure.

Photographs and Captions

How do the photographs and caption relate to the text?

_____

_____

_____

Reread

Author's Craft

How is it helpful that the author begins this section by mentioning the microscopes you use at school?

The light microscopes you use in school are weak and do not show much detail. An electron microscope is a much more powerful tool. It allows scientists to see things we can't see with our eyes, such as skin cells or dust mites.

The picture below is a close-up of human skin and shows the detail an electron microscope can capture. The more an image is magnified, the more detail you will see. The most magnification that a photomicrograph can capture is about 2 million times the original image size.

Magnified images have helped scientists to see what causes diseases. Over the years, scientists have learned how these diseases behave. We have even learned what is inside a cell or how a snowflake **dissolves** into a drop of water.

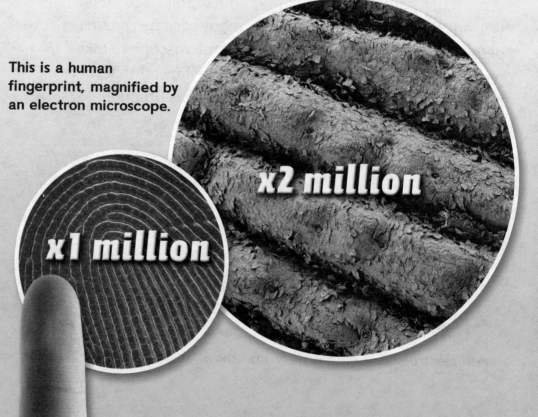

This is a human fingerprint, magnified by an electron microscope.

x1 million

x2 million

(l) 123ducu/iStock/Getty Images; (c) Clouds Hill Imaging Ltd./Corbis Documentary/Getty Images; (r) Clouds Hill Imaging Ltd./Corbis

When the mold on a strawberry is looked at under an electron microscope, it resembles grapes.

Scientists use electron micrographs to see how objects change over time. For example, we can look at a piece of fruit to see how it decays. First the fruit looks fresh. After a few days, it will soften. Specks of mold will appear and **cling** to it. Days pass and it will be covered in mold. A microscope shows this far earlier than our eyes.

Suppose you **mingle** with friends outside on a **humid** day. What would the sweat on your skin look like magnified? The possibilities are endless if you examine your world up close.

(l) Petals and posies/Alamy; (r) NaturePics/Alamy Stock Photo

Summarize

Use your notes and the photos and captions to help you orally summarize "Your World Up Close." Talk about whether your prediction on page 2 was confirmed.

FIND TEXT EVIDENCE

Read

Paragraphs 1–2

Sequence

Draw a box around the words that tell you when fruit begins to soften.

Antonyms

Underline an antonym for *decays*. Use context clues to help you figure out the meaning of *decays*.

Reread

Author's Craft

How does the author use sequence to show how useful electron microscopes can be?

Fluency

Take turns reading the first paragraph on page 5 to a partner. Make sure you read the question and statement sentences with the proper expression.

Vocabulary

Use the example sentences to talk with a partner about each word. Then answer the questions.

cling

A monkey can **cling** to a tree branch with its long arms.

What can a sticky note cling to?

_____

_____

dissolves

A sugar cube **dissolves** quickly in hot water.

What is something else that dissolves in water?

_____

_____

gritty

The sand on my feet feels **gritty**.

What other things feel gritty?

_____

_____

humid

The air is **humid** on rainy summer days.

What is a synonym for _humid_?

_____

_____

magnify

Let's **magnify** a leaf to see its details up close.

How are the words _magnify_ and _enlarge_ similar?

_____

_____

Build Your Word List Pick one of the interesting words you noted on page 2 and look up its meaning. Then work with a partner to write three sentences using the word: a statement, a question, and an exclamation.

microscope

The scientist used a **microscope** to look at tiny plant cells.

What would you like to view through a microscope?

_____

_____

mingle

Penguins **mingle** and socialize on the ice.

Who do you like to mingle with?

_____

_____

typical

Cold, snowy weather is **typical** here in winter.

What is typical summer weather in your region?

_____

_____

Antonyms

As you read "Your World Up Close," you may come across a word that you don't know. Look for context clues. Sometimes the author will use an **antonym**, a word or phrase that means the opposite of the unfamiliar word.

🔍 FIND TEXT EVIDENCE

I'm not sure what huge _means in this sentence on page 3:_ "The sugar crystal on the left may look huge, but the word _micro_ means small." _I can use the word_ small _to help me figure out what_ huge _means._

The sugar crystal on the left may look huge, but the word _micro_ means small. We are seeing a small part of the sugar crystal up close.

Your Turn Use context clues and antonyms to figure out the meanings of these words in the selection.

unique, page 3 _____

_____

weak, page 4 _____

_____

_____

Zoonar RF/Getty Images

Summarize

To summarize a paragraph or a whole selection, retell the main ideas or details in your own words. Reread "Your World Up Close" and summarize sections of the text to make sure you understand them.

 FIND TEXT EVIDENCE

Reread the fourth paragraph on page 3. Identify and summarize the key details in the paragraph.

Quick Tip

After you read a paragraph, write down the most important details. When you finish reading a page, read all your notes. This will help you summarize the whole selection.

Page 3

Photomicrography dates back to 1840, when a scientist named Alfred Donné first photographed images through a microscope. Around 1852, a German pharmacist made the first version of a camera that took photomicrographs. In 1882, Wilson "Snowflake" Bentley of Vermont became the first person to use a camera with a built-in **microscope** to take pictures of snowflakes. His photographs showed that there is no such thing as a **typical** snowflake. Each is unique. Nowadays, we have electron micrographs.

In 1882, Wilson Bentley was the first person to get close-up pictures of snowflakes. He used a camera attached to a microscope. His photographs showed each snowflake is unique.

 Your Turn Reread page 5 and summarize the key details. As you read, list the main ideas and details. Then retell them in your own words.

_____

_____

_____

Photographs and Captions

"Your World Up Close" is an expository text. An expository text

- gives facts and information about a topic
- includes text features, such as photographs and captions

🔍 FIND TEXT EVIDENCE

I can tell that "Your World Up Close" is an expository text. It gives facts and information about electron microscopes. It also has photographs and captions about things a microscope can see. These text features help me better understand the text.

Readers to Writers

Writers use photographs and captions to give readers a deeper understanding of a topic. Photographs help readers see what the words in the text describe. Captions explain the photographs and may give readers extra facts about the topic. How can you use these text features in your own writing?

Page 5

When the mold on a strawberry is looked at under an electron microscope, it resembles grapes.

Scientists use electron micrographs to see how objects change over time. For example, we can look at a piece of fruit to see how it decays. First the fruit looks fresh. After a few days, it will soften. Specks of mold will appear and **cling** to it. Days pass and it will be covered in mold. A microscope shows this far earlier than our eyes.

Suppose you **mingle** with friends outside on a **humid** day. What would the sweat on your skin look like magnified? The possibilities are endless if you examine your world up close.

Summarize

Use your notes and the photos and captions to help you orally summarize "Your World Up Close." Talk about whether your prediction on page 2 was confirmed.

Photographs and Captions

Photographs help to illustrate information described in the text. Captions explain the photographs and add other important information about the topic.

Your Turn Find and list two text features in "Your World Up Close." Tell your partner what information you learned from each of the features.

_____

_____

_____

_____

_____

Sequence

Authors use text structure to organize information in a text. **Sequence** is one kind of text structure. Authors use a sequential text structure to present information in time order. In a sequential text structure, authors use words that signal time, such as *first, then,* and *after.*

 FIND TEXT EVIDENCE

On page 5 of "Your World Up Close," I read how fruit decays over time. I will look for signal words, such as first *and* after.

First the fruit looks fresh.

↓

After a few days, it will soften.

↓

Days pass and the fruit is covered in mold.

Quick Tip

To find the sequence, or time order, of things, look for what happened first, next, and last. Words such as *first, then, next, before, after, yesterday, today, tomorrow,* and *later* tell you when things happen. To identify sequence, ask yourself as you read, *When does this event take place?*

 Your Turn Reread page 3 of "Your World Up Close." Fill in your graphic organizer with details about the development of photomicrography.

Respond to Reading

COLLABORATE

Discuss the prompt below. Think about how the author presents the information. Use your notes and graphic organizer.

How does the author's use of text structure and text features help you understand how electron microscopes help scientists?

_____

_____

_____

_____

_____

_____

_____

_____

_____

_____

_____

_____

Quick Tip

Use these sentence starters to discuss the text and organize your ideas.

- _The author explains that first . . ._
- _The author shows how . . ._
- _The author helps me understand why . . ._

Grammar Connections

As you write your response, remember these rules to help you make comparisons:

- When comparing two things, use _more_ before adjectives with two or more syllables: _Your microscope is **more powerful** than mine._

- When comparing three or more things, use _most_ before adjectives with two or more syllables: _This new microscope is the **most powerful** ever built._

Reading a Diagram

Authors use diagrams to present information in a visual form. A **diagram**

- shows the parts of something or how a process works
- includes labels or captions that identify each part

To read a diagram, follow the lines or arrows that point to each part. Read the label by each part. The labels describe the parts in the diagram.

The diagram to the right shows the life cycle of a butterfly. What does a caterpillar become? Write your answer.

_____

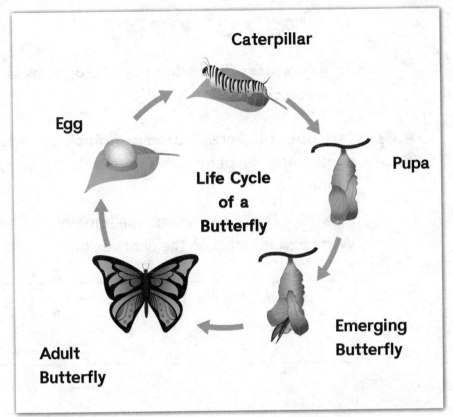

Caterpillar

Egg

Life Cycle of a Butterfly

Pupa

Emerging Butterfly

Adult Butterfly

Make a Diagram With your partner, make a research plan to study the sequence of the water cycle. Use a variety of sources. Then:

- Make a diagram of the water cycle.
- Use labels, descriptions, and arrows to show how the process works.

With your partner, discuss your research plan and the sources you will use with a librarian or other adult. As you take notes, paraphrase the information instead of copying it directly. Using other people's ideas and words without giving them credit is called "plagiarism." Think about what you want to use to make your diagram.

If you follow the arrows and read the labels, it will help you understand the stages, or parts, of the life cycle of a butterfly. What does a butterfly do to continue the cycle? Write your answer below.

_____

_____

snapgalleria/Shutterstock.com

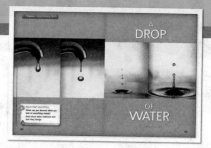

A Drop of Water

How does the author use photographs to help explain complex ideas?

Literature Anthology:
pages 362–379

COLLABORATE

Talk About It Reread **Literary Anthology** page 364. Then analyze the photographs on page 365. Turn to your partner and describe what is happening.

Cite Text Evidence How do the photographs and text go together? Write text evidence in the chart below.

 Make Inferences

When you reread the text, you can gather evidence to help you make inferences. What can you infer will happen if you put a teaspoonful of lemonade mix in a glass of water?

What the Text Says	→	What the Photos Show
	→	
	→	
	→	
	→	

Write The photos support the text because _____

_____

_____

_____

? How does the author use a blue drop of water to explain how water becomes ice?

Talk About It Reread the first paragraph on **Literary Anthology** page 366. Turn to your partner and talk about what happens to the blue drop when it becomes ice.

Cite Text Evidence How does the author help you understand the difference between the molecules in liquid water and ice? Write text evidence in the diagram.

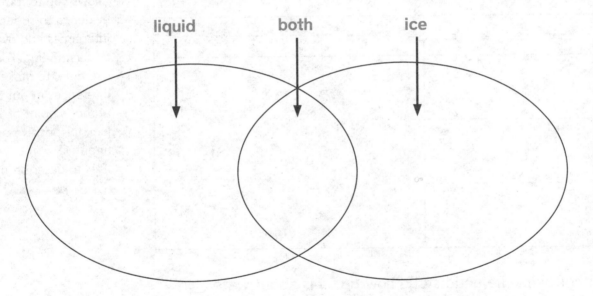

liquid   both   ice

Write The author uses a blue drop of water to explain how water becomes ice because _____

_____

_____

_____

Quick Tip

When you reread, picture in your mind what the author is describing. For example, picture the blue drop of water freezing into ice.

Synthesize Information

When you read, combine what you already know with new information in the text. For example, combine what you already know about water and ice with what you learn about water molecules in the text. Think about the drop of blue water discussed in the text. How would the selection be different if the author did not include a photo of it?

How does the author help you understand how he feels about water?

COLLABORATE

Talk About It Reread the last paragraph on **Literary Anthology** page 379. Turn to your partner and discuss why the author says that water is precious.

Cite Text Evidence What reasons does the author provide to help you understand his point of view about water? Write text evidence in the chart.

Text Evidence	Author's Point of View

Write The author helps me understand how he feels about water _____

_____

_____

_____

_____

Quick Tip

To find the author's point of view, look for clues that reveal the author's opinion of the topic.

Make Inferences

Reading the text carefully allows you to gather evidence to support your inferences and overall understanding. For example, to make inferences about the author's point of view, look for positive or negative words the author uses to describe the topic.

Respond to Reading

Discuss the prompt below. Apply your own knowledge about water to inform your answer. Use your notes and your graphic organizer to help you.

Why does the author begin and end the selection with a drop of water?

_____

_____

_____

_____

_____

_____

_____

_____

_____

_____

_____

Santasan/Shutterstock.com

Quick Tip

Use these sentence starters to organize your text evidence.

- *The author begins and ends the selection with a drop of water because . . .*
- *The author explains the water cycle because . . .*

Self-Selected Reading

When you read independently, you read on your own. Set aside some time to read for an extended period of time. This will help you develop a personal connection to texts and topics you are interested in.

Choose a text. Read the first two pages. If five or more words are unfamiliar, pick another text. Fill in your writer's notebook with the title, author, and genre. Record your purpose for reading.

The Incredible Shrinking Potion

Literature Anthology: pages 382–385

1 It began as a simple science project.

2 It was only one week ago that Isabel, Mariela, and Hector were working on a shrinking potion that would amaze everyone at the science fair. Mariela and Isabel had perfected the potion, but it was Hector who had created the antidote. Since his discovery, Hector had become less interested in winning the science fair prize and more interested in how this experiment could increase his popularity. His short stature made him practically invisible to everyone at Washington Elementary School.

3 That wasn't the case anymore—now the entire class was looking up at Hector. He had come to the science lab bearing "special" cupcakes, which made it easy for him to shrink the entire class, including his science teacher, Ms. Sampson. Hector smirked as he placed his miniature classmates inside the tank of Rambo, the class pet.

Reread paragraph 2. How does the author help you understand why Hector shrinks his classmates? **Make marks** by two sentences that explain Hector's motivation. Write them here.

_____

_____

_____

_____

COLLABORATE

Talk with a partner about what kind of character Hector is. **Circle** words the author uses to describe Hector and his actions.

4 Isabel and Mariela overheard the shrinking shrieks of their classmates outside the classroom door. The girls had been late to lab again. Upon peering inside, they quickly realized they had to do something. Mariela saw that Rambo, outfitted with a vest of tiny tubes, was sniffing merrily outside his tank.

5 "Rambo has the antidote!" Mariela whispered. "We will have to shrink ourselves to sneak inside and get the antidote. Then we can help everyone out of the tank!" With shaking hands, Isabel pulled out a vial. The girls took a deep breath and sipped the shrinking potion. The world around them began to grow . . . .

6 As Isabel and Mariela walked under the classroom door, everything was magnified to the extreme. Desks and chairs towered over them— even the complex details of each nut and screw became clear, as if viewed under a microscope. The girls made their way to the other side of the lab, dodging mountainous cupcake crumbs and wads of gooey gum.

Reread paragraphs 4 and 5. **Draw a box** around the words the author uses to describe what Isabel and Mariela see and hear outside of their classroom door.

COLLABORATE

Reread paragraph 6. Talk about what the girls see when they walk under the classroom door.

Underline descriptive words the author uses to help you picture what Isabel and Mariela see. Write them here:

_____

_____

_____

? **How does the author use words and phrases to help you visualize what the classroom looks like to Isabel and Mariela?**

Talk About It Reread the excerpt on page 19. Talk with a partner about why Mariela and Isabela take the shrinking potion.

Cite Text Evidence What words does the author use to describe the classroom from Isabel and Mariela's point of view? Write text evidence in the chart.

Quick Tip

When you reread, ask yourself these questions.

• *Which words tell about the sights and sounds in the setting? Which words describe the actions or feelings of the characters?*

Use these sensory details to help you visualize the scene in your mind.

Text Evidence	What I Visualize

Write The author helps me visualize what Isabel and Mariela see by

_____

_____

asiseeit/E+/Getty Images

Imagery

Imagery is the use of words to help readers visualize what the author is describing. Authors use sensory words to show what things look, sound, feel, taste, or smell like. Sensory words help readers to create a picture in their minds of what is happening.

FIND TEXT EVIDENCE

On page 383 in the **Literature Anthology**, the author of "The Incredible Shrinking Potion" uses sensory words to help readers visualize the gigantic objects. The author's imagery helps readers picture what it looks and feels like to move around giant crumbs and wads of sticky gum.

> The girls made their way to the other side of the lab, dodging mountainous cupcake crumbs and wads of gooey gum.

Your Turn Reread the first paragraph on page 384.

- What words does the author use to help you visualize the table?

_____

_____

- What words does the author use to help you visualize what Isabel is doing and feeling? _____

_____

When you write, visualize the setting, characters, and actions. Then use your five senses to describe all the sights, sounds, smells, tastes, and feelings in the scene. If you use sensory words, your readers will be able to clearly paint pictures in their minds. These mental pictures help readers enjoy the adventure right along with the characters.

Text Connections

Courtesy National Gallery of Art, Washington

? How do the photographer and the authors of the "How Old Is Your Water" Blast, *A Drop of Water,* and "The Incredible Shrinking Potion" help you understand what you can discover when you look at things closely?

Talk About It Read the caption and look at the series of photographs. Talk with a partner about how the photographer broke the horse's motions into smaller parts.

Cite Text Evidence Circle a part in each photograph that changes from one frame to the next.

Write The Blast, Eadweard Muybridge's photographs, *A Drop of Water*, and "The Incredible Shrinking Potion" help me to

_____

_____

_____

_____

_____

_____

_____

Quick Tip

Observe how the photographer helps you to look closely at the way a horse runs. This will help you compare these photographs to the texts.

Eadweard Muybridge was a famous photographer who took pictures of many animals and people in motion. This series of photographs is called "Animal Locomotion, Plate 626" and was created in 1887.

Present Your Work

Discuss how you and your partner will present your water cycle diagram to the class. You may want to plan a digital slide presentation or display the diagram on the wall. Use the Presenting Checklist as you rehearse your presentation, and offer and accept feedback.

The most interesting thing I learned about the water cycle is _____

_____

_____

I would like to know more about _____

_____

Quick Tip

Plan your presentation with your partner. Divide your tasks. Agree on who will talk first. Practice, so you know what to say and how long the presentation will take. Leave time for questions.

Presenting Checklist

☐ Speak slowly, clearly, and with expression.

☐ Make eye contact with the audience.

☐ As you explain each stage in the water cycle, point to it on your visual.

☐ Listen carefully to questions from the audience.

☐ Listen politely to any questions and suggestions.

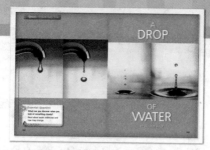

*Literature Anthology:
pages 362-379*

Expert Model

Features of an Explanatory Essay

An explanatory essay is a form of expository text. It informs readers about a topic by presenting facts and information. An explanatory essay

- summarizes information from a variety of reliable sources

- categorizes, or groups together, related information

- uses linking words to connect ideas

Word Wise

On page 364, author Walter Wick uses *is not, it has,* and *would not* instead of *isn't, it's,* or *wouldn't.* This helps to give his writing a formal tone. The purpose of an explanatory essay is to inform readers, or help them learn about a topic. So it should have a formal tone.

Analyze an Expert Model Studying expository texts will help you learn how to write an explanatory essay. **Reread** page 364 of *A Drop of Water* in the **Literature Anthology**. Write your answers below.

What is the main idea of this section of the text? _____

_____

_____

List two examples of linking words or phrases the author uses to connect ideas on this page.

1 _____

2 _____

Plan: Choose Your Topic

Brainstorm With a partner or a small group, brainstorm a list of objects (living things or nonliving things) you think would be interesting to see up close or learn more about.

_____

_____

_____

Writing Prompt Choose one object from your list. After researching your object, you will write an explanatory essay about it. Describe what you discovered about the object when you closely observed it.

I will write about _____

Purpose and Audience An **author's purpose** is his or her main reason for writing. Look at the three purposes for writing below. Underline your purpose for writing an explanatory essay.

to inform, or teach   to persuade, or convince   to entertain

Think about the audience for your explanatory essay. Who will read it? My audience will be _____

I will use _____ language when I write my essay.

Plan In your writer's notebook, make a Main Idea and Details chart to plan your essay. Write your topic in the "Main Idea" box. Then, in the other boxes, list details that support that main idea.

Quick Tip

To help you plan for a certain audience, ask yourself these questions.

- _What do the people already know about my topic?_

- _What more do they need to know?_

- _How can I make them see what I see when I look at this object up close?_

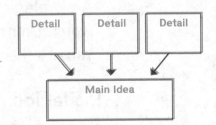

Plan: Take Notes

Research Before you begin to write, research information from two reliable sources. Some reliable digital and print sources are: encyclopedias, museums, universities, and government sites. Skim and scan your two sources to make sure they have enough information on your topic.

List the two sources you will use in your research. For each source, note the title, author's name, name of the website or publisher, the publication date, and the page number.

1 _____

2 _____

Take Notes As you reread your sources, record your notes on your Main Idea and Details chart. To take notes, you should:

• Ask questions: What do I need to know about my topic?

• Find the answers from your two sources.

• Avoid plagiarism by paraphrasing, or writing the answers in your own words. Do not copy the exact words from a source, unless you use them in a quote.

┌─ **Digital Tools** ──────────────────────────
For more information on how to take notes, watch the
"Take Notes: Print" tutorial. Go to **my.mheducation.com**.
└───

Marc Romanelli/Blend Images

Draft

Categorize Information The author of an explanatory essay groups related information into paragraphs. Each paragraph includes a topic sentence that gives the main idea of the paragraph. Details in the other sentences clearly relate to that main idea. In the example below from "Your World Up Close," the main idea is that magnified images have helped scientists. The other sentences in the paragraph relate to how magnified images help scientists.

> <u>Magnified images have helped scientists</u> to see what causes diseases. Over the years, scientists have learned how these diseases behave. We have even learned what is inside a cell or how a snowflake dissolves into a drop of water.

Now use the above paragraph as a model to write about the topic you chose. Remember to group only ideas related to the main idea of your paragraph.

_____

_____

_____

 Write a Draft Use your Main Idea and Details chart to help you write your draft in your writer's notebook. Make sure each paragraph focuses on one topic and the details in that paragraph relate to that topic.

Grammar Connections

Remember to use the correct punctuation when you refer to your sources in your essay. Use italics or underlining for the title of a book, magazine, or newspaper:

- *In the magazine <u>Animal World</u>, the author writes. . .*

Use quotation marks around the title of a print or online article or the chapter of a book:

- *According to the article "Bee Careful!" bees are. . .*

Revise

Linking Words Effective writers use linking words and phrases to help readers understand the relationships between ideas. Some common linking words and phrases are: *and, also, but, so, because, finally, first, next, although, as a result,* and *therefore*. Read the paragraph below. Then revise it to add linking words that connect ideas.

> Bees live in colonies. One bee is queen. The others are worker bees. Worker bees collect pollen. This helps feed the colony. The pollen helps plants to grow. Some pollen from the flower sticks to the bee's body. The bee leaves some of the pollen on the next flower. This helps more plants to grow. The bee flies the rest of the pollen home.

Quick Tip

When you revise, check that you have a variety of sentences. If you have a lot of short sentences, use linking words to combine sentences. For example, these two short sentences could be combined: *Bees drink nectar from flowers. Pollen sticks to their bodies.* You can join them with linking words: *When bees drink nectar from flowers, pollen sticks to their bodies.*

_____

_____

_____

_____

Revision Revise your draft, and check that you have linking words or phrases to help your reader connect ideas. Make sure you have paraphrased (used your own words) or give proper credit for any quoted words.

Tomasz Pietryszek/E+/Getty Images

Peer Conferences

COLLABORATE

Review a Draft Listen carefully as a partner reads his or her work aloud. Take notes about what you liked and what was difficult to follow. Begin by telling what you liked about your partner's draft. Ask questions that will help your partner think more carefully about his or her writing. Make suggestions that you think will make the writing more focused and coherent. Use these sentence starters.

I like that you group all the facts about . . .

The linking words you use help me . . .

I'm not sure this part belongs here. Can you explain why . . .?

Partner Feedback After your partner gives you feedback on your draft, write one of the suggestions that you will use in your revision. Refer to the rubric on page 31 as you give feedback.

Based on my partner's feedback, I will _____

_____

_____

After you finish giving each other feedback, reflect on the peer conference. What was helpful? What might you do differently next time?

Revision As you revise your draft, use the Revising Checklist to help you figure out what text you may need to add, delete, combine, or rearrange. Remember to use the rubric on page 31 to help with your revision.

Revising Checklist

- [ ] Are related details grouped into paragraphs?
- [ ] Are ideas presented in a logical order?
- [ ] Are linking words used to connect ideas?
- [ ] Is there a variety of sentences that help make the writing interesting?
- [ ] Are content words used correctly?
- [ ] What can I add or subtract to make my explanation clearer?

Edit and Proofread

When you **edit** and **proofread** your writing, you look for and correct mistakes in spelling, punctuation, capitalization, and grammar. Reading through a revised draft multiple times can help you make sure you're catching any errors. Use the checklist below to edit your sentences.

✓ Editing Checklist

☐ Do all sentences begin with a capital letter and end with a punctuation mark?

☐ Does every sentence have a subject and predicate?

☐ Are source titles listed correctly?

☐ Are commas used correctly?

☐ Are comparative adjectives used correctly?

☐ Are all words spelled correctly?

Grammar Connections

If you quote a text, remember these rules:

- Copy the exact words from the text.

- Put quotation marks around the whole quote.

- Tell who wrote the quote. For example: *In the book* Bees Everywhere, *Dr. Rivera writes, "Bees are hardworking."* (Notice the comma before the first quotation mark and the end punctuation inside the second quotation mark.)

List two mistakes you found as you proofread your essay.

1 _____

_____

2 _____

_____

Publish, Present, and Evaluate

Publishing When you **publish** your writing, you create a clean, neat final copy that is free of mistakes. Write your final draft in cursive, holding your pen or pencil between your forefinger and thumb. Consider adding visuals—such as drawing illustrations or including pictures you download from the Internet—to help make your essay more interesting.

Presentation When you are ready to **present** your work, rehearse your presentation. Use the Presenting Checklist to help you.

Evaluate After you publish your writing, use the rubric below to **evaluate** your writing.

What did you do successfully? _____

What needs more work? _____

_____

✔ **Presenting Checklist**

☐ Stand or sit up straight.

☐ Look at the audience.

☐ Speak clearly and loud enough for everyone to hear you.

☐ Use a friendly but formal tone.

☐ Answer questions from the audience thoughtfully.

4	3	2	1
• an engaging explanation of a single topic, with strong focus for the purpose and task • information is grouped in paragraphs according to topic with key details • consistent use of linking words	• a clear explanation of a single topic, which focuses mostly on the purpose and task • information is mostly grouped in paragraphs according to topic • adequate use of linking words	• main idea of a topic somewhat unclear and focus lacks purpose and task • many details are not grouped in paragraphs according to topic • inconsistent use of linking words	• main idea confusing or lacking focus of the purpose and task • most details are not grouped in paragraphs according to topic • few or no linking words

Talk About It

People show that they care about each other in different ways. Look at the photograph. How does the boy show that he cares about the other person?

What are some ways you show you care about your friends and family?

Talk with a partner about what you can do to help others. Remember to make eye contact as you speak. Enunciate and speak slowly and clearly. Write your ideas in the chart.

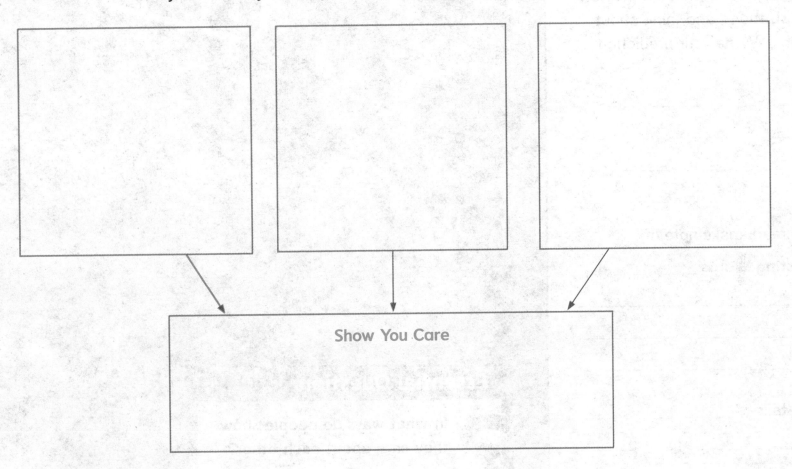

Show You Care

Go online to **my.mheducation.com** and read the "Lending a Helping Hand" Blast. Think about how you can use your hobbies to help others. Then blast back your response.

hana/Datacraft/Getty Images

SHARED READ

PREVIEW AND MAKE PREDICTIONS

To help you focus as you read, preview the text and make a prediction about what will happen in the story. Read the title, preview the illustrations, and think about the genre. Write your prediction below.

_____
_____
_____
_____

As you read, make note of:

Interesting Words _____

_____
_____
_____

Key Details _____

_____
_____
_____

Sadie's Game

Essential Question

In what ways do people show they care about each other?

Read how a brother shows that he cares about his little sister.

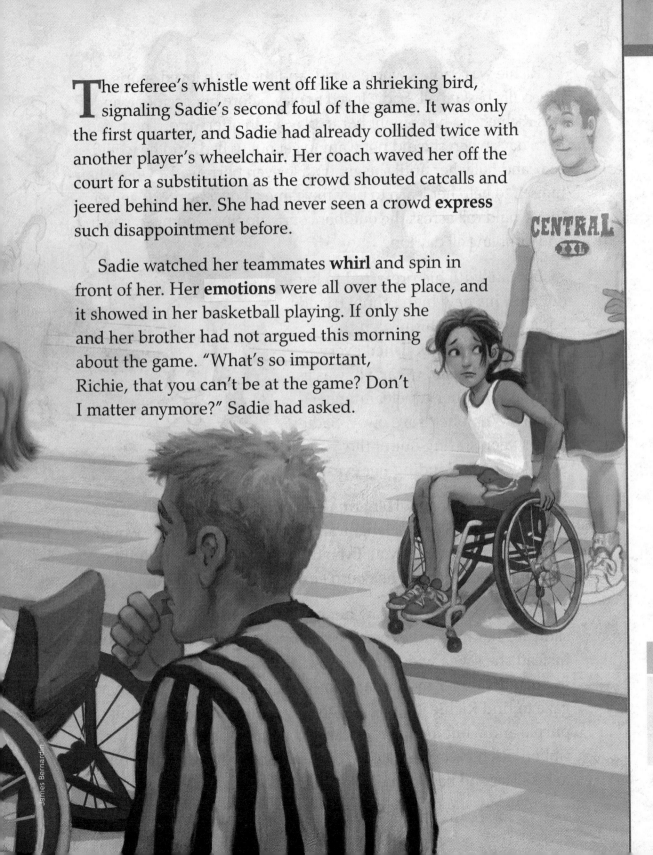

The referee's whistle went off like a shrieking bird, signaling Sadie's second foul of the game. It was only the first quarter, and Sadie had already collided twice with another player's wheelchair. Her coach waved her off the court for a substitution as the crowd shouted catcalls and jeered behind her. She had never seen a crowd **express** such disappointment before.

Sadie watched her teammates **whirl** and spin in front of her. Her **emotions** were all over the place, and it showed in her basketball playing. If only she and her brother had not argued this morning about the game. "What's so important, Richie, that you can't be at the game? Don't I matter anymore?" Sadie had asked.

REALISTIC FICTION

FIND TEXT EVIDENCE

Read

Paragraph 1
Visualize

Underline the text that helps you visualize the actions of Sadie, the coach, and the crowd.

Paragraph 2
Problem and Solution

Draw a box around the problem between Sadie and Richie. Write the problem on the line.

_____

_____

Foreshadowing

Circle a sentence that gives a clue that Sadie's relationship with Richie will change.

Reread

Author's Craft

How does the author's use of the words *whirl* and *spin* help describe Sadie's teammates?

FIND TEXT EVIDENCE

Read

Paragraphs 1–2

Problem and Solution

Draw a box around the problem Sadie had after her accident. Write on the line how Richie helped her solve that problem.

_____

_____

Paragraphs 3–4

Similes and Metaphors

Circle the two things compared in paragraph 3. Is the comparison a simile or a metaphor?

_____

Visualize

Underline the words and phrases that help you picture the actions of Sadie's mother.

Reread

Author's Craft

How does the author show that the relationship between Sadie and her brother has changed?

Richie was Sadie's whole world, and they both loved sports, especially basketball. Sadie loved to play before her accident, and it was Richie who had taught her to play again afterward. There had been days when she did not want to get out of bed, and he would coax and bully her until she got up. He even borrowed a wheelchair himself to help her learn to play the game all over again. Together they would roll across the outdoor court, zipping, zooming, passing, and dribbling all day long.

But lately Richie preferred to hang out with his new high school friends. Sadie would watch through the window as Richie polished every little nook of his new car. He was as **fussy** as a mother cat cleaning her kittens. When he drove away, Sadie would keep staring out of the window, tears clouding her eyes.

Mama was her sun. Her arms would reach out and **encircle** her in a long, warm embrace. "Sadie," she would say, "your brother loves you. Even though he's got new priorities now, that doesn't mean he doesn't care." But Sadie felt hurt.

Sadie looked up and saw her coach frowning. She searched sadly for her mother, expecting disappointment in her eyes, but instead she saw a wide smile. It was the same happy face she saw in **portraits** of her mother at home. Sadie followed her mother's gaze to find Richie jogging toward her across the gym, holding a purple and white **bouquet** of flowers wrapped tightly with a ribbon. Richie's eyes **sparkled,** and his smile gleamed. He bowed to his sister and handed her the flowers as though she were a queen.

"But we're losing. How do you know we're going to win?" she asked.

"I don't," Richie said. "It's not important. What I know is you're like a whirlwind on the court, and there is no way I am going to miss my little sister's big game!" He put his hand on her shoulder as he said, "It's great to have a lot of new friends, but I realized that you're my best friend."

Sadie smiled. Those words meant more to her than "I'm sorry" ever could. She rested the flowers on her lap and went back out onto the court. Right then Sadie decided to play the rest of the game with the bouquet in her lap. With her brother watching from the sidelines, Sadie stole the ball from an opponent and dribbled her way to the net, making the first of what would be many amazing shots for the team.

Summarize

Use your notes and the illustrations to write a summary of the events in "Sadie's Game." Say whether your prediction on page 34 was confirmed.

James Bernardin

FIND TEXT EVIDENCE 🔍

Read

Paragraphs 1–3

Similes and Metaphors

Circle the simile in paragraph 2. What two things are compared?

_____

_____

Evaluate Information

Underline what Richie says to help Sadie feel better about their relationship. Why was this better than saying, "I'm sorry"?

_____

_____

_____

_____

Reread

Author's Craft

How does the author use the setting to help solve Sadie's problem with her brother?

Vocabulary

Use the example sentences to talk with a partner about each word. Then answer the questions.

bouquet

I gathered the beautiful flowers into a **bouquet**.

How does a bouquet look, smell, and feel?

_____

_____

emotion

Sadness is an **emotion** you may feel when you move away from your friends and neighborhood.

What is an emotion you felt today?

_____

_____

encircle

The children held hands to **encircle** the tree.

How are the words _encircle_ and _surround_ similar?

_____

_____

express

The child made a picture of a rainbow to **express** his love of color.

What would you express in your picture?

_____

_____

fussy

Fussy Mr. Green stood in front of the mirror until his bow tie looked perfect.

What is a synonym for _fussy_?

_____

_____

Build Your Word List Underline a word that looks interesting to you. Use print or digital resources to look up its meaning. Write the word and its meaning in your writer's notebook. Then look up and make a list of synonyms for the word.

portraits

This week students in Ann's art class are drawing **portraits** of each other.

What portraits might you see hanging in the White House?

_____

_____

sparkled

The gold beaded curtain **sparkled** in the light.

Name some other things that sparkle.

_____

_____

whirl

The dancers were able to **whirl** and twirl without getting dizzy.

What is a synonym for _whirl?_

_____

_____

Similes and Metaphors

Literal language is the dictionary definition of a word. Figurative language, such as simile and metaphor, gives words different meanings to appeal to the reader's senses. A **simile** uses the words _like_ or _as_ to compare two things. A **metaphor** compares two or more things without using the words _like_ or _as_.

FIND TEXT EVIDENCE

I see a simile in the first sentence of "Sadie's Game" on page 35, shown below. In this sentence, the sound of the whistle is compared to a noisy bird.

The referee's whistle went off like a shrieking bird, signaling Sadie's second foul of the game.

Your Turn Find the similes and metaphors listed below. Tell what is being compared in each. Then identify if it is a simile or a metaphor.

"Richie was Sadie's whole world," page 36

_____

"He was as fussy as a mother cat cleaning her kittens," page 36 _____

Visualize

When you read, picture the characters, key events, and setting of the story. As you read "Sadie's Game," stop and visualize events to help you better understand the story.

🔍 **FIND TEXT EVIDENCE**

After reading page 36 of "Sadie's Game," I can use the details to picture the events described in the story.

Quick Tip

Words and phrases that help describe the five senses are called sensory details. Remember, your five senses are seeing, hearing, feeling, smelling, and tasting. Authors use sensory details to help readers picture the story they are reading.

Page 36

But lately Richie preferred to hang out with his new high school friends. Sadie would watch through the window as Richie polished every little nook of his new car. He was as **fussy** as a mother cat cleaning her kittens. When he drove away, Sadie would keep staring out of the window, tears clouding her eyes.

I visualize Sadie staring out the window with tears in her eyes as her brother drives off in his car. This helps me understand Sadie's feelings.

Your Turn Reread the last paragraph on page 36 of "Sadie's Game." Visualize how Richie looks as he jogs toward Sadie. What words in the text help you picture the scene? As you read, remember to use the strategy Visualize.

_____

_____

Foreshadowing

"Sadie's Game" is realistic fiction. Realistic fiction is a made-up story with realistic characters, events, and setting. It has dialogue and may contain literary elements, such as foreshadowing. Realistic fiction can be told in the first-person or third-person point of view.

🔍 FIND TEXT EVIDENCE

I can tell "Sadie's Game" is realistic fiction because Sadie is a character who could exist in real life. Also, the setting and events are believable. The story is told by a narrator in the third-person point of view and includes foreshadowing.

Page 36

Mama was her sun. Her arms would reach out and **encircle** her in a long, warm embrace. "Sadie," she would say, "your brother loves you. Even though he's got new priorities now, that doesn't mean he doesn't care." But Sadie felt hurt.

Sadie looked up and saw her coach frowning. She searched sadly for her mother, expecting disappointment in her eyes, but instead she saw a wide smile. It was the same happy face she saw in **portraits** of her mother at home. Sadie followed her mother's gaze to find Richie jogging toward her across the gym, holding a purple and white **bouquet** of flowers wrapped tightly with a ribbon. Richie's eyes **sparkled**, and his smile gleamed. He bowed to his sister and handed her the flowers as though she were a queen.

Foreshadowing

Foreshadowing gives clues to show what will happen next in a story without giving the action away. When Sadie looks up at her mother and sees her smiling, the author is giving the reader a clue that something good is about to happen.

Your Turn Find and list two other examples from the story that show that "Sadie's Game" is realistic fiction. Then identify another example of foreshadowing in the story.

_____

_____

_____

_____

In a third-person point of view, the narrator shares the thoughts and feelings of one character or of several characters. Writers use the pronouns *he, she, they*.

In a first-person point of view, the story is told by a character, using the pronouns, *I, we, us, our*.

Problem and Solution

Identifying the **problem** and **solution** in a story can help you understand the characters, setting, and plot. The problem is what the characters want to do, change, or find out. The solution is how the problem is solved.

🔍 FIND TEXT EVIDENCE

As I read pages 35–36, I can see Sadie has a problem. I will list the key events in the story. Then I can figure out how Sadie finds a solution.

> **Characters**
> Sadie, Richie, Sadie's mother

⬇

> **Setting**
> A basketball court

⬇

> **Problem**
> Sadie is playing badly. She is upset that Richie did not come to the game.

Your Turn Reread "Sadie's Game." Fill in the graphic organizer on page 43. Identify the characters, setting, and problem. Then find two important story events and list them under "Events." Use the story events to identify the solution. Write the solution in the "Solution" box.

id="1"

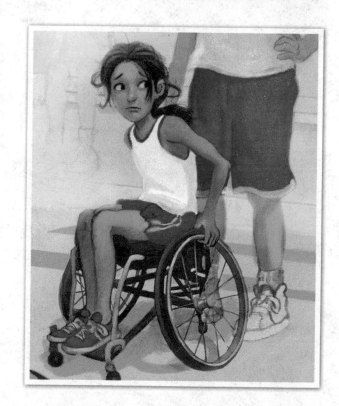

Quick Tip

Quick Tip

Remember, characters are the people or animals in a story. The characters usually have a problem that needs to be solved. The setting is where and when they solve the problem. To find the problem in a story, you can ask: *What went wrong?* To find the solution, you can ask: *How did the characters fix the problem?*

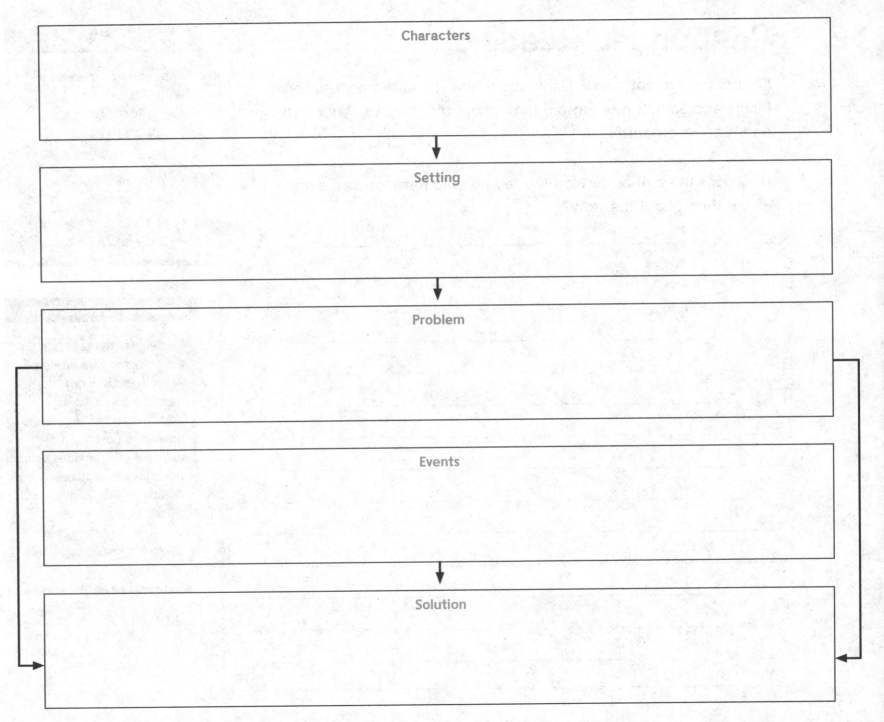

Characters

Setting

Problem

Events

Solution

Respond to Reading

Discuss the prompt below. Think about how the author focuses on Richie and Sadie's relationship throughout the story. Use your notes and graphic organizer.

How does the author develop the relationship between Sadie and Richie throughout the story?

_____

_____

_____

_____

_____

_____

_____

_____

_____

_____

_____

_____

Quick Tip

Use sentence starters to help you organize your text evidence.

- *In the beginning of the story, Sadie is . . .*

- *In the middle of the story, Sadie is . . .*

- *By the end of the story, Sadie and Richie . . .*

Grammar Connections

Remember to use adjectives in your writing. Adjectives are words that describe nouns. Most adjectives come before the noun they describe. For example: *The* **anxious** *sister waits for her brother.* Adjectives are usually placed in order of *opinion, size, age,* and then *color*: *There is a lovely, huge, old, blue house.*

Make a Research Plan

When you do a research project, make a plan. A **research plan** helps you organize your notes and stay on topic. Here are some things to include in your plan:

- An inquiry chart tells what you already know about the topic, what you want to find out, and the key words and key phrases to use for your search.
- Write a list of research questions about your topic in the middle column of the chart. In your questions, ask: *Who? What? Where? When? Why?* and *How?*

Write a sample research question below.

_____

_____

INQUIRY CHART		
What I Know About My Topic	What I Want to Find Out About My Topic	Key words and Key Phrases

Create a Poster for a Cultural Festival With a partner or small group, research different cultural celebrations in your state. Choose one that interests you.

- Make an inquiry chart and fill in the three columns.
- Ask your teacher or a librarian to help you with your research questions.
- Take notes about the history, customs, and foods associated with the celebration.
- Make a print or digital poster for a cultural festival for the celebration.
- Include pictures and information on the poster.
- Share your poster with your classmates.

Lane Oatey/Getty Images

Mama, I'll Give You the World

 How does the author use figurative language to help you understand Mama and Luisa's relationship?

Literature Anthology: pages 386–401

 Talk About It Reread the first two paragraphs on page 390 of the **Literature Anthology**. Turn to your partner and talk about how the author describes Mama and Luisa.

Cite Text Evidence What metaphors tell you about Mama and Luisa? Write text evidence in the chart.

Figurative Language	What Does This Show?

Write The author uses figurative language to show that _____

_____

_____

 Synthesize

Use what you learned about descriptive language to create a new understanding. Describe what a bouquet of flowers is like. Use sensory words to tell what a bouquet looks like, how it smells, and what it feels like. Compare how people can be like a bouquet of flowers.

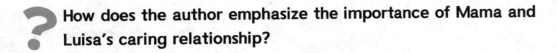

? **How does the author emphasize the importance of Mama and Luisa's caring relationship?**

Talk About It Reread page 394 of the **Literature Anthology**. Turn to a partner and talk about what Luisa and Mama say to each other. What do they mean when they say they want to give each other the world?

Cite Text Evidence What words and phrases show that Mama and Luisa care about one another? Write text evidence in the chart.

	What They Think or Say	What They Do
Mama		
Luisa		

Write The author emphasizes the importance of Mama and Luisa's

relationship by _____

_____

Quick Tip

You can use these sentence starters to show how Mama and Luisa care about each other.

- *Mama wants to give Luisa the world by . . .*
- *Luisa wants to give Mama the world by . . .*
- *I can tell how Luisa feels when she says . . .*

Make Inferences

The author does not always tell the reader everything about a character or event in the story. Authors give clues to help the reader infer, or make logical decisions, about the story characters and events. What do the story clues tell about the kind of person Mama is?

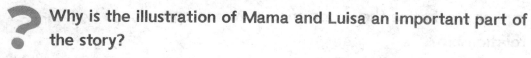

? Why is the illustration of Mama and Luisa an important part of the story?

Talk About It Reread the last paragraph on page 398 of the **Literature Anthology**. Look at the illustration on page 399. Turn to your partner and talk about how the illustration helps you visualize the moment.

Cite Text Evidence How does the illustration connect to what you read? Write text evidence in the chart.

Illustration Clues	How It Connects

Write The illustration of Mama and Luisa is an important part of the story because _____

_____

_____

_____

Quick Tip

Illustrations show parts of a story. Readers can connect the words in the story with the illustrations. Look at the gestures and expressions of the characters. The illustrations help readers to see what the characters look like and how they feel.

 Evaluate Information

How do the illustrations in the story help you understand the characters, setting, and events? Flip through the story and look at the illustrations. Which illustration helps you understand the story best? How does the illustration help you? What does the illustration help you understand?

Respond to Reading

COLLABORATE

Discuss the prompt below. Think about how the author focuses on Mama and Luisa's relationship throughout the story. Use your notes and graphic organizer.

Quick Tip

Use sentence starters to help you organize your text evidence.

- *The author shows how Mama and Luisa . . .*
- *By choosing this title, the author . . .*
- *The illustrations show . . .*

Why is *Mama, I'll Give You the World* a good title for this story?

Miami by Way of Fujian

[1]   Sometimes, I wonder who I really am.

[2]   You're thinking, Hey, Mariel, you're a short fifth-grade girl with straight black hair and almond eyes. You live in Miami. I know where my family comes from.

[3]   My *abuelos* talk about Cuba: the pristine beaches and smooth jazz bands. So when my mom told me we were going to visit where I came from, for a moment I imagined a village in Cuba.

[4]   "No, *mi vida*. We're going to China to see where you were born." Her voice trembled with emotion as we got on the plane . . .

[5]   The flight to Hong Kong lasted twenty hours! The city amazed me. How could so many people crowd onto the sidewalks? Many people had black straight hair and almond eyes like mine. . . .

[6]   The next day we took a flight to Fuzhou. After the flight, there was an all-day car ride to the village. Mami smiled while she cried. She was remembering when they had first come to the orphanage to adopt me.

Literature Anthology
pages 404–407

Reread paragraphs 1–4. **Underline** the words and phrases in paragraph 2 that tell you how Mariel describes herself. **Draw a box** around where Mariel thinks she is going to visit in paragraph 3. Write why Mariel wonders who she really is.

_____

_____

_____

_____

COLLABORATE

Reread paragraph 5. Talk with a partner about why Mariel is amazed by Hong Kong. **Circle** the text evidence that supports your discussion.

1   . . . The nursery had white walls, and the floor was covered with soft foam puzzle pieces that looked like giant marshmallows. A row of wheeled bassinets lined a wall, where an older woman rocked a crying baby. When she saw us she spoke excitedly.

2   Ms. Guo translated. "Xing Hua can't believe how big you are." Ms. Guo led us to a classroom jammed with kids. The teacher wrote on the board in English. After the lesson, the kids raced to the playground for recess. A girl about my age hung back. She was shorter than me and her hair was tied in ponytails.

3   I asked, "What's your name?"

4   "Mei Jing."

5   "Are you the oldest here?"

6   "Yes, I'm ten years old."

7   I had a million questions but I didn't want to be pushy. She hesitated and then asked me, "Is your school fun? Do you like it?"

8   "Sure. What about you?"

9   "Yes. But I want to go to school in the city, with older children."

10   I felt bad for Mei Jing. I hoped that one day she would find parents.

Reread paragraphs 1–10 with your partner. **Underline** the sentence that tells why Mariel feels bad for Mei Jing.

COLLABORATE

Look at the glossary. Discuss the words and their meanings with your partner.

Glossary

Abuela: grandmother
Abuelos: grandparents
Arroz salteado: fried rice
Bai cai: bok choy, a type of cabbage
Chica China: a Chinese girl
Dim sum: dumplings and other small dishes served from carts
Fujian: location on the southeast coast of mainland China
Kowloon: a dense urban area in Hong Kong
Mi vida: "My life"—a term of endearment

Which words are nouns that name people?

_____

_____

Which words are nouns that name places?

_____

? **What inferences can you make about the kind of person Mariel is?**

Reread the excerpts on pages 50 and 51. Discuss how the author describes Mariel. Think about Mariel's words and actions.

Cite Text Evidence Reread the dialogue between Mariel and Mei Jing. What story clues does the author give about the kind of person Mariel is? Write the text evidence in the chart.

Quick Tip

Writers do not always directly tell readers everything that takes place in a story. Instead, writers may give story clues or details to help readers make inferences, or figure out things for themselves.

For example, a writer might describe a boy's stomach as grumbling and making a lot of noise. And a writer might include an illustration with a clock that reads 12:00. The reader can infer from the story clues that the boy is hungry.

Story Clues

↓

↓

↓

↓

Inference

Write By describing Mariel and her conversation with Mei Jing, the author _____

_____

Make Inferences

Sometimes writers do not always tell readers everything that takes place in a story. Writers give story clues or details so the readers can figure out things for themselves. When you **make an inference,** you use story clues to make a logical decision about the characters, setting, or plot.

🔍 FIND TEXT EVIDENCE

On page 50 in "Miami by Way of Fujian," the author provides clues about how Mariel's mom feels about the trip to China. The author doesn't tell how Mariel's mom feels. Instead, the author writes that the mother's voice trembles with emotion as they got on the plane. This hints that the trip will bring back joyful memories of when Mariel was adopted.

> "No, *mi vida*. We're going to China to see where you were born."
> Her voice trembled with emotion as we got on the plane.

Your Turn Read paragraphs 1–6 on page 51.

• What inferences can you make about how Xing Hua feels about Mariel?_____

_____

• What inferences can you make about how Mei Jing feels about Mariel?

_____

_____

Readers to Writers

If you want your readers to make inferences, include enough clues or details. Use describing words to tell about characters and settings. You can use dialogue to tell how a character feels about something without showing what the person is really like.

Text Connections

? How does Edwin Markham use figurative language to describe how the character feels? How is Markham's use of language similar to the way the authors use language in *Mama, I'll Give You the World* and "Miami by Way of Fujian"?

Talk About It With a partner, read the poem. Talk about what the speaker does and how it makes him feel.

Cite Text Evidence **Underline** words and phrases in the poem that help you visualize how the speaker feels. **Circle** how you know doing something nice for someone made the speaker feel good.

Write Edwin Markham's use of figurative language is like

_____

_____

_____

_____

_____

_____

_____

_____

Comstock Images/Alamy

Quick Tip

The figurative language in the poem helps you understand the poet's feelings. This will help you compare the poem to the selections you read this week.

Two at a Fireside

I built a chimney for
a comrade old,
   I did the service not
for hope or hire—
And then I traveled on
in winter's cold,
   Yet all the day I glowed
before the fire.

      — Edwin Markham

Present Your Work

Discuss how you will present your poster about a cultural festival to the class. Use the checklist as you practice your presentation. Discuss the sentence starters below and write your answers.

An interesting fact I learned about the cultural celebration is _____

_____

_____

I would like to learn more about _____

_____

_____

Quick Tip

Before presenting your poster, be sure the text is readable and the images are large enough for people to see. Point to the text and images as you present the poster.

✔ Presenting Checklist

- ☐ Practice sharing your poster in front of a friend. Ask for feedback.
- ☐ Speak clearly, with appropriate expression and a slow pace.
- ☐ Explain why you included the facts and images on the poster.
- ☐ Listen carefully to questions from the audience.

Efrain Padro/Alamy Stock Photo

Talk About It

Essential Question

How can learning about the past help you understand the present?

COLLABORATE

Archaeologists search for artifacts that explain how people lived long ago. These clues to the past tell us about the foundations of our country and other countries. Why is learning about the past important? How can it help us understand the present? Write words that describe why the past is important. Then talk with a partner about a period of history you would like to learn about, and explain why.

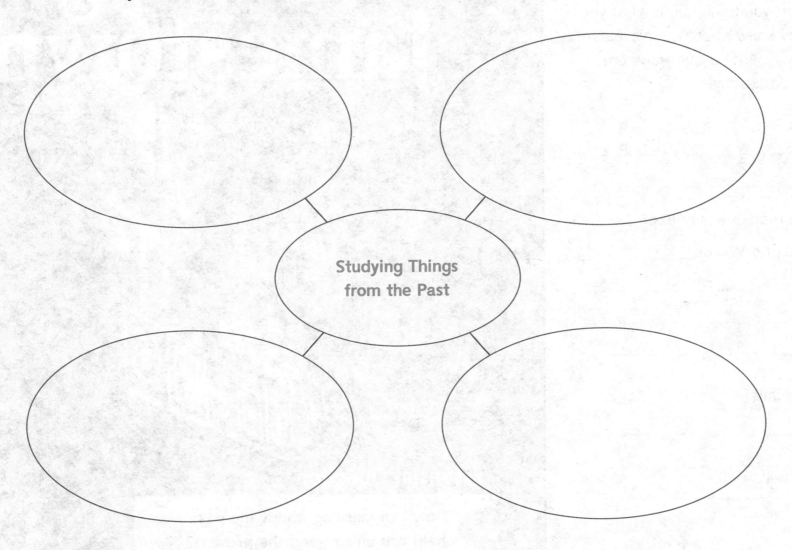

Studying Things from the Past

BLAST BACK!
studysync

Go online to **my.mheducation.com** and read the "Live and Learn" Blast. What would you hope to dig up if you were an archaeologist? Blast back your response.

Jeffrey Rotman/Corbis Documentary/Getty Images

TIME
FOR KIDS.

The Founding of Jamestown

TAKE NOTES

Asking questions helps you figure out your purpose for reading. It also lets you think about what you already know about a topic. Before you read, write a question here about Jamestown.

_____

_____

_____

As you read, make note of:

Interesting Words _____

_____

_____

_____

Key Details _____

_____

_____

_____

_____

_____

Essential Question

? How can learning about the past help you understand the present?

Read about the Jamestown settlement.

Ed George/National Geographic/Getty Images

The building of the Jamestown settlement in 1607

North Wind/North Wind Picture Archives

Take a tour of Jamestown.

They thought they were lost. The *Susan Constant*, the *Godspeed*, and the *Discovery* had sailed from London, England, on December 20, 1606. The **expedition** was bound for Virginia, carrying 144 people.

Finally, on April 26, 1607, the ships sailed into Chesapeake Bay. In the words of one voyager, they found "fair meadows and goodly tall trees." Later, on an island in a river, they built a fort and named it after their king, James. Jamestown would become the first successful, **permanent** English settlement in the New World.

The Struggle to Survive

There is a proverb that says, "Ignorance is bliss." In the case of the 104 men and boys who came ashore, this was true. They were faced with **tremendous** challenges. The water from the James River was not safe to drink, and food was scarce. The Native Americans resented the settlers for taking their land.

FIND TEXT EVIDENCE 🔍

Read

Paragraphs 1-2

Sequence

Underline what the voyagers did after they found "fair meadows" by Chesapeake Bay.

Paragraph 3

Summarize

Circle key details you would use to summarize the challenges the settlers faced when they came ashore. Write a summary below.

_____

_____

_____

_____

_____

_____

Reread

Author's Craft

How does the illustration on this page help you to better understand the selection?

FIND TEXT EVIDENCE

Read

Paragraphs 1-2

Sequence

Draw a box around the detail that tells what John Smith was before he became head of Jamestown. Write when John Smith became the head of Jamestown.

_____

Sidebar

Underline why Pocahontas never returned to Jamestown. Write below why John Smith admired Pocahontas.

_____

_____

Reread

Author's Craft

What was the author's purpose for including a sidebar about Pocahontas?

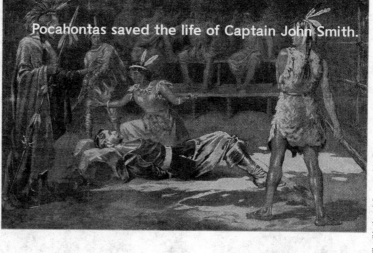

Pocahontas saved the life of Captain John Smith.

(t) Classic Image/Alamy Stock Photo; (b) W. Langdon Kihn/National Geographic Creative/Alamy Stock Photo

John Smith, an experienced military man, became head of the colony in 1608. He had been in charge of finding local tribes willing to swap food for English copper and beads. Smith was tough with both the Indians and Englishmen. "He that will not work, shall not eat," he told the colonists. Smith knew that an attitude of every man for himself would endanger the colony.

The western Chesapeake area was ruled by Chief Powhatan, who governed an empire of 14,000 Algonquian-speaking peoples. His daughter Pocahontas became a useful friend and ally to John Smith.

The Real-Life Pocahontas

Princess Matoaka was born around 1595. Her father, Chief Powhatan, called her Pocahontas. She saved John Smith's life twice, and he wrote that Pocahontas's "wit and spirit" were unequaled.

Pocahontas married a planter named John Rolfe, the first marriage in that **era** between an Englishman and a Native American woman. Rolfe, Pocahontas, and their son visited London. She never returned home—she fell ill aboard a ship bound for Jamestown in March 1617 and died.

The map at the top of the page:

Map Key
- Recreation of 1600s brick foundation
- Site of 1600s archaeological remains
- Pitch and tar swamp
- Walkway

Labels on map: Voorhees Archaearium Archaeology Museum, Statehouse, OLD TOWNE, Tercentenary Monument, Pocahontas Statue, 1607 James Fort, John Smith Statue, Governor Harvey House, Governor Harvey Property (Industrial Area), Rowhouse, Memorial Church, Historic Tower, Bland Warehouse, Marable House/Workshop, NEW TOWNE, Merchant Rowhouse, JAMES RIVER

(t) Mapping Specialists; (c) Courtesy of APVA Preservation Virginia

Taking a Closer Look

Archaeologists digging in Jamestown have discovered Indian artifacts along with English ones, **evidence** that Indians lived in the fort for some time. "It must have been a very close relationship," says William Kelso, an expert in colonial American **archaeology**.

Kelso has worked for 10 years to **document** this site. His team has managed to **uncover** more than 1 million artifacts and has mapped out the fort's shape, its foundations, and a burial ground.

Jamestown left a record of greed and war, but it was also the start of representative government. On July 30, 1619, the first representative assembly in English North America met in the Jamestown church.

Dr. William Kelso working on the archaeological dig in Jamestown

Summarize

Use your notes, the sidebar, and the map to help you summarize "The Founding of Jamestown" for a partner. Talk about whether you found the answer to the question you asked on page 58.

FIND TEXT EVIDENCE

Read

Paragraphs 1–3

Summarize

Underline the things in paragraph 1 that archaeologists discovered at Jamestown. **Circle** what they learned from their discoveries.

Map

Look at the map. **Circle** James Fort. **Draw a box** around the part of town it is in.

Proverbs and Adages

How does the proverb "Nothing ventured, nothing gained" relate to the founding of Jamestown?

_____

_____

_____

Reread

Author's Craft

How does the author help you understand that Jamestown is still important today?

Vocabulary

Use the example sentences to talk with a partner about each word. Then answer the questions.

archaeology

In **archaeology** class, Ana studied ancient objects from Egypt.

How does archaeology help us to learn about the past?

_____

_____

document

Ming keeps a diary to **document** every day of his vacation.

How would you document your vacation?

_____

_____

era

The moon landing in 1969 was the beginning of a new **era** in space exploration.

What invention ended the era of the horse and buggy?

_____

_____

evidence

The detectives looked for **evidence** at the crime scene.

Why do detectives look for evidence?

_____

_____

expedition

A scientist led an **expedition** to explore the rain forest.

Where would you like to lead an expedition?

_____

_____

Build Your Word List Pick one of the interesting words you noted on page 58 and look up its meaning in a print or digital dictionary. Then use the word in two sentences: a statement and a question. Share your sentences with a partner.

permanent

Loud noises can cause **permanent** damage to your hearing.

What is an antonym for *permanent*?

_____

tremendous

I had a **tremendous** amount of homework last weekend!

What is a synonym for *tremendous*?

_____

_____

_____

uncover

We dug up the dirt to **uncover** the buried treasure.

What might you uncover if you lift a big rock?

_____

_____

_____

Proverbs and Adages

Proverbs and adages are sayings that have been used for a long time and express a general truth. Look for context clues to figure out their meanings.

🔍 FIND TEXT EVIDENCE

In the section "The Struggle to Survive" on page 59, I see the proverb Ignorance is bliss. *The phrases* tremendous challenges *and* food was scarce *help me to figure out what the proverb means.*

There is a proverb that says, "Ignorance is bliss." In the case of the 104 men and boys who came ashore, this was true. They were faced with tremendous challenges. The water from the James River was not safe to drink, and food was scarce.

Your Turn Use context clues to determine the meaning of the following adage from the selection.

"He that will not work, shall not eat," page 60

_____

_____

_____

North Wind/North Wind Picture Archives

Summarize

To summarize, retell the key ideas or details briefly in your own words. Reread "The Founding of Jamestown" and summarize sections of the text to make sure you understand the important information.

 FIND TEXT EVIDENCE

Reread the sidebar "The Real-Life Pocahontas" on page 60. Summarize the most important information.

Quick Tip

As you read, stop often to summarize, or review, the part you just read. Write the most important information on sticky notes. Then, read on and stop to summarize other parts of the text. At the end, read your sticky notes. This will help you remember and understand what you read.

> Page 60
>
> Princess Matoaka was born around 1595. Her father, Chief Powhatan, called her Pocahontas. She saved John Smith's life twice, and he wrote that Pocahontas's "wit and spirit" were unequaled.
>
> Pocahontas married a planter named John Rolfe, the first marriage in that era between an Englishman and a Native American woman. Rolfe, Pocahontas, and their son visited London. She never returned home—she fell ill aboard a ship bound for Jamestown in March 1617 and died.

Pocahontas was a famous Native American woman. She was the daughter of Chief Powhatan and saved John Smith's life twice. She was the first Native American woman to marry an Englishman.

 Your Turn Reread the section "Taking a Closer Look" on page 61 of "The Founding of Jamestown." Summarize the most important details.

_____

_____

_____

_____

Sidebars and Maps

"The Founding of Jamestown" is an expository text.

An **expository text**

- is nonfiction
- provides information and facts about people, places, and things
- may include text features, such as maps and sidebars

FIND TEXT EVIDENCE

I can tell "The Founding of Jamestown" is an expository text because it gives facts about the history of Jamestown and about the people who lived there. The sidebar and map provide more information, too.

Readers to Writers

Writers use sidebars to highlight interesting facts related to a topic. Writers include maps to show the location of places in the text. Both sidebars and maps help readers better understand the main text. You can use sidebars and maps to give more specific details about the topic in your writing.

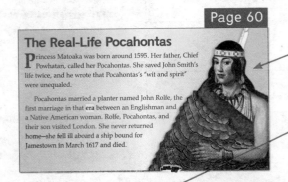

Page 60

The Real-Life Pocahontas

Princess Matoaka was born around 1595. Her father, Chief Powhatan, called her Pocahontas. She saved John Smith's life twice, and he wrote that Pocahontas's "wit and spirit" were unequaled.

Pocahontas married a planter named John Rolfe, the first marriage in that **era** between an Englishman and a Native American woman. Rolfe, Pocahontas, and their son visited London. She never returned home—she fell ill aboard a ship bound for Jamestown in March 1617 and died.

Page 61

Sidebar
A sidebar contains additional information.

Map
A map shows a specific geographical area.

Your Turn Reread "The Founding of Jamestown." Find two other text features. Tell what information you learn from each feature.

_____

_____

_____

Sequence

Text structure is the way authors organize and present information in a selection. **Sequence** is one kind of text structure. Authors present key events in the order in which they happened. Look for dates and words that signal time.

 FIND TEXT EVIDENCE

When I reread page 59 of "The Founding of Jamestown," I can look for dates and sequence words, such as finally, next, *and* later *to understand the order of the events in the text.*

> Three ships sailed from London in 1606.

> Finally, the ships sailed into Chesapeake Bay in 1607.

> Later, on an island in a river, they built a fort and named it after their king, James.

 Your Turn Reread "The Real-Life Pocahontas" on page 60. List the key events in time order in the graphic organizer on page 67.

Quick Tip

Look for words, phrases, and dates that signal the sequence of events. Writers use words such as *first, next, finally, later, before,* and *after* to order events. Ask yourself, "When is this event happening?" Write each event on a sticky note. Then draw a line on a sheet of paper and place the sticky notes on it to create a timeline.

Respond to Reading

COLLABORATE

Discuss the prompt below. Think about how the author presents the information. Use your notes and graphic organizer.

How does the author use text features to help you understand the importance of Jamestown?

_____

_____

_____

_____

_____

_____

_____

_____

_____

_____

_____

_____

Quick Tip

Use these sentence starters to organize your ideas.

- *The author uses illustrations, photos, and captions to show . . .*
- *The sidebar tells . . .*
- *The map shows . . .*

Grammar Connections

Check your writing for run-on sentences. A run-on sentence joins two or more complete sentences with no punctuation or the wrong punctuation. A comma splice is a type of run-on sentence that joins two complete sentences with a comma. For example, *Pocahontas saved John Smith's life, he praised her.* To correct the comma splice, add the conjunction *and. Pocahontas saved John Smith's life, and he praised her.*

Map and Map Key

A **map** is a detailed drawing that shows the surface features of an area, such as a town, state, or country. Some maps show geographical regions, such as mountains, plateaus, valleys, and coastal plains. Most maps have a **map key** that shows what the different colors or symbols on the map represent. To read a map and understand all the details, you should:

- Read the map title.
- Study the map key carefully.
- Match the information on the map key to the colors on the map.

What place would you like to make a map of? Write it here.

_____

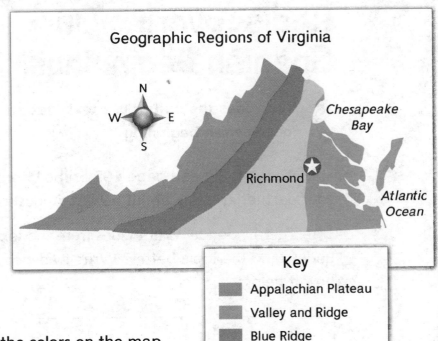

Geographic Regions of Virginia

Chesapeake Bay

Richmond

Atlantic Ocean

Key

- Appalachian Plateau
- Valley and Ridge
- Blue Ridge
- Piedmont
- Coastal Plain

COLLABORATE

Make a Map With a partner, research where the Spanish established settlements in the Southwest in the 1700s. Then create a map to show the different regions with Spanish settlements at that time. On your map, be sure to include important features, such as

- symbols for the settlements
- major rivers, mountains, or other geographical features
- names of towns

Make sure your map has a map key and a title to help readers understand what they are seeing. Finally, share your work with the class.

The map above shows geographic regions of Virginia. What region lies between the Piedmont and Valley and Ridge regions? Write your answer below.

_____

_____

_____

Rediscovering Our Spanish Beginnings

Literature Anthology: pages 408–411

? How does the author use text features to help you understand our Spanish beginnings?

Talk About It Reread page 409 of the **Literature Anthology**. Turn to your partner and talk about how St. Augustine was founded.

Cite Text Evidence What clues from the text features help you understand the topic better? Write evidence in the chart and explain how it helps.

Illustrations and Captions	Heading	How the Text Features Help

Write The author's use of text features helps me to _____

_____

_____

Quick Tip

Illustrations with captions, headings, maps, photographs, and sidebars are text features. They can give more information about the topic and help you better understand the topic.

Make Inferences

Why did the Spanish king think it was unacceptable that France established Fort Caroline in 1564?

How does the author use sidebars to connect the past and present?

Talk About It Reread pages 410 and 411 of the **Literature Anthology**. Turn to your partner and talk about how the information provided in the sidebars supports the main text.

Cite Text Evidence What information do the sidebars add to your understanding of past and present Spanish influence? Write it in the web.

Quick Tip

When you reread, use the sidebar to help you find out even more about the topic. Ask yourself: *What new facts does the author give me? How does this new information relate to the main text?*

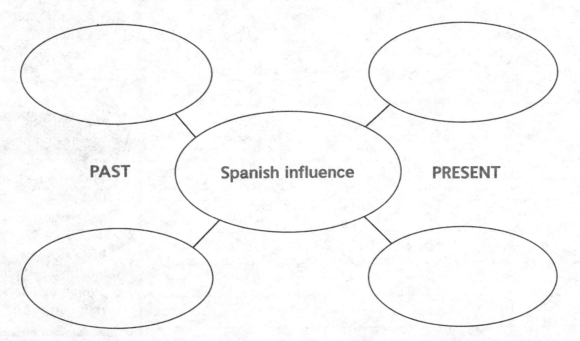

PAST   Spanish influence   PRESENT

Write The author uses sidebars to help me understand the connection between the past and present by _____

_____

_____

Respond to Reading

Discuss the prompt below. Apply your own knowledge of the topic, your notes, and your graphic organizers to help you.

How does the author's use of text features help you understand how history has shaped America's culture?

_____

_____

_____

_____

_____

_____

_____

_____

_____

_____

_____

_____

Quick Tip

Use these sentence starters to help organize your text evidence.

- *The author uses illustrations and photos to . . .*
- *The sidebars help me to understand . . .*
- *Together, all the text features help me to understand . . .*

Self-Selected Reading

Choose a text. Read the first two pages. If five or more words are unfamiliar, pick another text. Fill in your writer's notebook with the title, author, and genre, and your purpose for reading.

History's Mysteries

Literature Anthology:
pages 412–413

Finding Popham

[1] In 1607, a crew of 125 English colonists set out on an expedition. They landed on Maine's coast. They erected a small settlement and named it for its principal backer, Sir John Popham, and his nephew George. But the Popham Colony—England's first attempt at a New England settlement—didn't survive. One year later, the colonists boarded their ship and sailed home.

[2] For centuries, no one knew precisely where the colony had been. Then archaeologist Jeffrey Brain began excavating the area in 1994. After ten years of digging, Brain and his team uncovered traces of the colony's storehouse, a hearth (or floor of a fireplace), and stoneware fragments. Their work has helped unearth clues about the way the colony lived.

Reread and use the prompts to take notes in the text.

Make a mark in the margin beside the events in paragraph 1 that tell what the English colonists did in 1607.
Underline what happened to the colonists one year later.

COLLABORATE

Reread paragraph 2. Talk with a partner about what Jeffrey Brain found. **Circle** text evidence to support your discussion.

Draw a box around the dates and time order words that the author uses to highlight the importance of Brain's discovery. Write them here.

_____

_____

? **What does the author think about archaeology?**

Talk About It Reread the excerpt on page 73. Talk with a partner about why the author might have put so many dates and time order words in the selection.

Cite Text Evidence In what ways does the author's word choice help you understand what he thinks about archaeology? Write text evidence in the chart.

Text Evidence	Author's Point of View

Write I know how the author feels about archaeology because _____

_____

_____

krugloff/Shutterstock.com

Quick Tip

When you reread, look for words and phrases that help you understand what the author thinks.

Evaluating Information

Before writing an expository text, the author researches the topic to make sure that what he or she tells readers is true. *How can you check that the dates and facts in an expository text are correct?*

Author's Purpose

Every author has a purpose, or reason, for writing. The author may want to inform, persuade, or entertain readers. If the purpose is to **inform** readers about a topic, the author gives important facts about people and events. The author researches the facts and uses at least two reliable resources. The writing will give *who, what, when, where,* and *how* details. The author may also include photographs with captions, maps, and other text features to help readers learn more about the topic.

FIND TEXT EVIDENCE

On page 73 of "History's Mysteries," the author gives a series of facts telling when, who, where, and why.

> In 1607, a crew of 125 English colonists set out on an expedition. They landed on Maine's coast. They erected a small settlement and named it for its principal backer, Sir John Popham, and his nephew George.

Your Turn Reread the last paragraph on page 73.

• What is the author's purpose in the last paragraph?

_____

• What information does the author include to help you know his or her purpose? _____

_____

Readers to Writers

Before you write, decide if your purpose is to inform, entertain, or persuade. Identify your intended audience or reader. Then choose the best way to present your message in an expository text. Will you tell the facts in sequence or through causes and effects? Or would it be better to compare and contrast ideas, people, or events? Once you decide, use precise words to clearly convey your message to your readers.

Text Connections

How will learning about the history of the Serpent Mound, St. Augustine, and the Popham Colony help you understand the present?

Quick Tip

Think about what the archaeologists learned in this week's selections. This will help you compare them to the photograph of the Serpent Mound.

Talk About It Look at the photograph and read the caption. Talk with a partner about what the photograph of the Serpent Mound shows.

Cite Text Evidence Use a pencil to **trace around** the snake in the photo. **Underline** clues in the caption that tell why the mound is important. Think about how the photographer and authors of *Rediscovering Our Spanish Beginnings* and "History's Mysteries" help you understand how the past helps archaeologists understand the present.

Write The photographer and authors help me understand that the past helps explain the present by _____

_____

_____

_____

_____

_____

_____

The Serpent Mound, in Ohio, is a mound of earth in the shape of a long snake. It was declared a National Historic Landmark. Researchers and archaeologists believe the mound was built by an ancient culture. This photograph shows an aerial view of the 1,345-foot-long serpent.

©Richard A. Cooke/Corbis

Rate and Expression

When you read aloud an expository text, review the text for punctuation marks and look for unfamiliar words you need help pronouncing. Read aloud the article at a slow and steady **rate,** so listeners will understand the ideas in the text. To make the reading more interesting, read aloud important words and ideas with **expression.** Listeners will have a better understanding of the text, too.

Quick Tip

Before you start, make sure you know how to pronounce each word. Use a print or digital dictionary to find a word's pronunciation. Take your time when you read aloud. Look out for punctuation marks. Emphasize, or stress, the important words or ideas. Then you will be reading with expression.

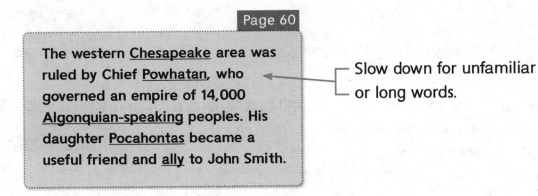

Page 60

The western <u>Chesapeake</u> area was ruled by Chief <u>Powhatan</u>, who governed an empire of 14,000 <u>Algonquian-speaking</u> peoples. His daughter <u>Pocahontas</u> became a useful friend and <u>ally</u> to John Smith.

Slow down for unfamiliar or long words.

COLLABORATE

Your Turn Take turns reading aloud "The Real-Life Pocahontas" on page 60. Record each other. Then listen to the playback. Did you read at a slow and steady rate? Did you pay attention to punctuation? Did you read some words or sentences with expression?

Afterward, think about how you did. Complete these sentences.

I remembered to _____

_____

Next time I will _____

_____

*Literature Anthology
pages 408–411*

Expert Model

Features of an Expository Essay

An **expository essay** informs readers by presenting ideas and facts about a topic. An expository essay

- presents information, facts, and details in a logical order

- includes text features, such as photographs, illustrations, captions, sidebars, or maps

- includes a strong conclusion that relates to the topic

Word Wise

On page 409, the author uses dates and words such as *begins, after, later, then,* and *a year later* to help order the information in the text. It is important to have a clear text structure like sequencing from the beginning to the end in an expository text.

Analyze an Expert Model Studying expository texts will help you learn how to write an expository essay. **Reread** page 409 of *Rediscovering Our Spanish Beginnings* in the **Literature Anthology**.
Write your answers below.

What is the main idea of the article? _____

_____

_____

What supporting details does the writer provide? _____

_____

_____

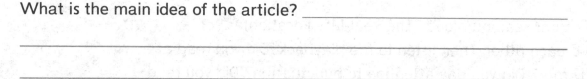

Alex Mares-Manton/Getty Imagesw

Plan: Choose Your Topic

Quick Tip

Talk with a partner about your ideas for organizing your essay. Decide which details you want to focus on as you write. Choose the details that support the main idea the best.

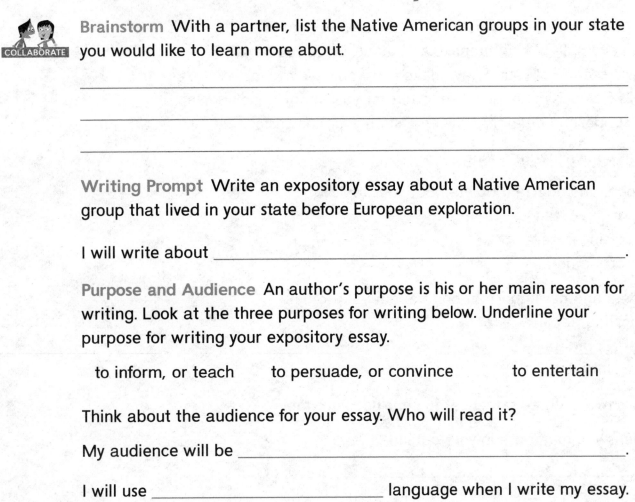

Brainstorm With a partner, list the Native American groups in your state you would like to learn more about.

_____

_____

_____

Writing Prompt Write an expository essay about a Native American group that lived in your state before European exploration.

I will write about _____.

Purpose and Audience An author's purpose is his or her main reason for writing. Look at the three purposes for writing below. Underline your purpose for writing your expository essay.

to inform, or teach   to persuade, or convince   to entertain

Think about the audience for your essay. Who will read it?

My audience will be _____.

I will use _____ language when I write my essay.

Plan In your writer's notebook, make a Main Idea and Supporting Details graphic organizer to plan your essay. Fill in the boxes.

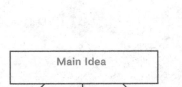

Plan: Write an Outline

Get Organized Make an outline to help you organize and plan your essay. Below is an example of how to make an outline. Once you have a main idea for each section of your essay, make sure you have at least two supporting details for each main idea. Use letters for your main ideas and numbers for the supporting details. At the end, state your conclusion.

Title: What you will write about

A. Main Idea: an important point about your topic
   1: supporting detail
   2: supporting detail
   3: supporting detail

B. Main idea: another important point about your topic
   1: supporting detail
   2: supporting detail
   3: supporting detail

Conclusion: two or three sentences to conclude your topic

List two main ideas you might use in your outline.

1 _____

2 _____

Take Notes On the Internet, research facts about the Native Americans you will be writing about. Look for two reliable sources to make sure the facts are accurate. Then use your graphic organizer to make a list of your main ideas and details. Include only the key details that support the main idea in each section, or paragraph.

Draft

Supporting Details Writers use supporting details to tell about a topic. The details may be facts, definitions, quotations, or examples about the topic. Details should support the main idea of the paragraph. In the example below from "The Founding of Jamestown," the author uses details that support the main idea about John Smith.

> John Smith, an experienced military man, became head of the colony in 1608. He had been in charge of finding local tribes willing to swap food for English copper and beads. Smith was tough with both the Indians and Englishmen. "He that will not work, shall not eat," he told the colonists. Smith knew that an attitude of every man for himself would endanger the colony.

Now use the above passage as a model to plan your expository essay. In the first sentence, give the name of the Native American group you chose to write about. Then include details about the group in your essay.

_____

_____

_____

 Write a Draft Use your Main Idea and Details graphic organizer to help you write your draft in your writer's notebook. Choose interesting facts or examples as supporting details.

Grammar Connections

Remember to use a capital letter to begin each proper noun, such as the name of a person, place, or Native American group. Other proper nouns, such as languages, names of races, and nationalities, should also be capitalized.

If you are using a direct quotation, remember to use quotations marks around the exact words in the quote.

Revise

Strong Conclusions A **strong conclusion** summarizes the main ideas in your essay. It tells how the main ideas are connected. The conclusion should be just a few sentences or a short paragraph. Strong conclusions leave a reader thinking about the topic, so ask yourself, "How can I make sure readers remember what I told them?" Read the paragraph below. Then add a sentence to make a stronger conclusion.

Quick Tip

When you revise your draft, you may need to add words to make smoother transitions. For example, use transition words and phrases such as *however, next, as a result,* and *finally.*

> The Algonquin are a Native American group in New York. They were important to our area before European explorers came. Archaeologists have explored sites of Algonquin settlements.

 Revision Revise your draft to improve your sentences by adding, deleting, combining, and rearranging ideas so they are clear to the reader.

Peer Conferences

Review a Draft Listen carefully as a partner reads his or her work aloud. Take notes about what you liked and what was difficult to follow. Begin by telling what you liked about the draft. Ask questions that will help the writer think more about the writing. Make suggestions you think will make the writing stronger. Use these sentence starters.

The beginning of your essay needs . . .

One more supporting fact you might add is . . .

This part is unclear to me. Can you explain what . . . ?

The conclusion can be made stronger by . . .

Partner Feedback After your partner gives you feedback on your draft, write one of the suggestions that you will use in your revision. Refer to the rubric on page 85 as you give feedback.

Based on my partner's feedback, I will _____

_____

_____

_____

After you finish giving each other feedback, reflect on the peer conference. What was helpful? What might you do differently next time?

Revision As you revise your draft, use the Revising Checklist to help you figure out what text you may need to move, elaborate on, or delete. Remember to use the rubric on page 85 to help with your revision.

Revising Checklist

- [ ] Do I begin with an introduction that gives the main idea of the topic?
- [ ] Does each paragraph have a main idea and supporting details?
- [ ] Do I present information in an organized way?
- [ ] Do I use precise words and formal language?
- [ ] Do I end with a strong conclusion?
- [ ] Do I have correct grammar and spelling, including correctly capitalized proper nouns?

Edit and Proofread

When you **edit** and **proofread** your writing, you look for and correct mistakes in spelling, punctuation, capitalization, and grammar. Reading through a revised draft multiple times can help you make sure you catch any errors. Use the checklist below to edit your sentences.

✔ Editing Checklist

- ☐ Do all sentences begin with a capital letter and end with a punctuation mark?
- ☐ Are all proper nouns capitalized?
- ☐ Is there subject and verb agreement?
- ☐ Do you use quotation marks correctly?
- ☐ Are there any run-on sentences?
- ☐ Are all words spelled correctly?

List two mistakes you found as you proofread your essay.

1 _____

_____

2 _____

_____

Grammar Connections

As you proofread your writing be sure to check that you have capitalized all the proper nouns. A proper noun names a particular person, place, or thing. Historical periods, events, documents, book titles, stories and essays, languages, races, and nationalities are all proper nouns. If you are not sure if a noun should be capitalized check an online reference source.

Publish, Present, and Evaluate

Publishing As you write your final draft, be sure to write legibly in cursive. Check that you are holding your pencil or pen correctly between your forefinger and thumb. This will help you to **publish** a neat final copy.

Presentation When you are ready to **present** your work, rehearse reading your essay aloud to a friend. Use the Presenting Checklist to help you.

Evaluate After you publish your writing, use the rubric below to **evaluate** your writing.

What did you do successfully? _____

What needs more work? _____

_____

✓ **Presenting Checklist**

☐ Stand up straight.

☐ Speak slowly and clearly.

☐ Use a friendly but formal tone.

☐ Pause to emphasize important points.

☐ Answer questions thoughtfully.

4	3	2	1
• gives an informative, interesting, and detailed explanation of the topic • provides main ideas and supporting details for each section • provides a clear introduction and a strong conclusion	• gives a detailed explanation about a topic • includes main ideas and some supporting details • has a satisfactory introduction and conclusion	• gives limited details about a topic • main ideas are not clear and there are very few supporting details • the introduction is missing details and the conclusion does not connect the main ideas	• does not focus on one topic • does not include enough main ideas and supporting details for each section • has a weak introduction and lacks a conclusion

Spiral Review

You have learned new skills and strategies in Unit 5 that will help you read more critically. Now it is time to practice what you have learned.

- **Antonyms**
- **Author's Purpose**
- **Make Inferences**
- **Photographs and Captions**
- **Plot**
- **Problem and Solution**
- **Proverbs and Adages**
- **Sequence**
- **Similes**

Connect to Content

- **Create a Digital Brochure**
- **Conduct a Magnet Experiment**

Read the selection and choose the best answer to each question.

Marvelous MAGNETS

1 People have known about magnets for thousands of years, and in the last century scientists have learned even more about them. Today, magnets are a major part of our everyday life. But how do magnets work and why are they so marvelous?

History

2 Today, people use magnets for a variety of reasons, but ancient people also used magnets. Ancient Greeks were among the first who discovered the power of magnets. In fact, the word *magnet* comes from the ancient Greek city Magnesia on the Maeander. The Vikings and the Ancient Chinese also knew about magnets. Ancient people used magnets to make compasses. Explorers used magnetic compasses to navigate their ships around the world.

What Are Magnets?

3 Most magnets are pieces of iron that attract other objects made of iron, nickel, or cobalt. Magnets come in a variety of shapes and sizes. You probably have used magnets in science class, but did you know that Earth is a huge magnet? Earth's core consists of molten rock, which is rich with iron. This iron creates a magnetic field that surrounds Earth. The magnetism stretches into space, too. Many of the other planets and the sun in the Milky Way solar system are magnets as well. However, Earth's moon is not a magnet.

nanantachoke/Shutterstock.com

This photo shows like poles repelling each other.

How Do Magnets Work?

4   Magnets have two poles: one north and one south. When like poles face each other, they repel, or push away. But when opposite poles face each other, they attract, or pull together. In other words, north poles attract south poles, but repel north poles. Every magnet is surrounded by a magnetic field. A magnetic field can attract or repel poles through air, water, and other magnetic objects.

How Does a Compass Work?

5   Compasses are one of the oldest practical uses of magnets. Why does a compass needle always point north? Earth's magnetic north pole attracts the compass needle. Once you know where north is, it is easy to find the other directions. You can make your own compass by hanging a bar magnet from a piece of string. The magnet will line up with Earth's magnetic field.

Electromagnets

6   The magnets you use in science class are <u>permanent</u> magnets. Electromagnets, however, are magnets that run on electricity. Their strength can change by the amount of electric current that runs through it. An electric current traveling through a wire produces a magnetic field around that wire. When the wire is wound into a coil around a magnet, the magnetic field is even stronger. Most of the appliances in your home, and even your electric toothbrush, use an electromagnet. On a larger scale, electromagnets generate most of the electricity we use today.

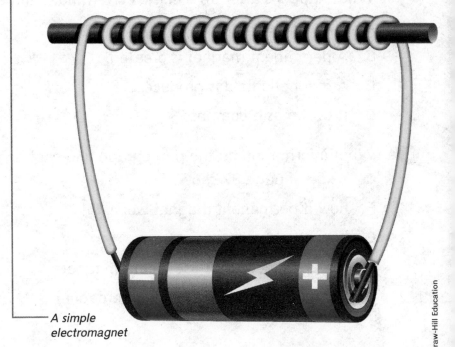

A simple electromagnet

McGraw-Hill Education

SHOW WHAT YOU LEARNED

1 The author's purpose for including paragraph 4 is to —

   A entertain about the ways people use magnets

   B explain to readers how magnets work

   C compare and contrast compasses to magnets

   D describe what horseshoe magnets look like

2 An antonym of the word <u>permanent</u> in paragraph 6 is —

   F temporary

   G magnetic

   H wired

   J reversible

3 What happens after an electric current flows through a wire?

   A The needle points to the north.

   B A permanent magnet is created.

   C A magnetic field is produced.

   D It becomes a compass.

4 What information do the photograph and caption on the bottom right side of page 87 show?

   F how a permanent magnet works

   G how an electromagnet works

   H the appliances that use electromagnets

   J the magnetic field of an electromagnet

Quick Tip

If you are not sure what a question is asking, you can underline details in the question. Then reread to find text evidence to answer it. Look at the photographs and captions. They help to explain important ideas in the text.

Read the selection and choose the best answer to each question.

Compass Campward -◄BOUND►-

1 "Ready to lose the Capture the Flag game again?" Lea asked Mr. Fath, her science teacher.

2 Mr. Fath smiled. "Sorry to disappoint you, but this is my team's year. I can feel it!"

3 Shaking her head, Lea said, "Our victory is going to be as sweet as pie!"

4 Every spring, fourth graders at Rockville Elementary went camping. Students were excited about the hiking and swimming, but most of all, they were thinking about Capture the Flag. Two teams had a hidden flag in each team's "territory." The first team to find their way through the woods and capture the other team's flag won. Last year, Lea's Team Orange won, and she was ready for a repeat performance.

5 "Ready, set, go!" shouted Mr. Fath.

6 Lea gathered Team Orange together before they headed out. Avery, Maria, Sophia, and Raoul huddled in a circle.

7 "We need to get that flag! Last year, we stayed together and worked as a team. Let's do that again."

8 Avery agreed, "We should definitely stick together like glue. And since this is our second time here, we'll be able to grab the flag with no problem!"

9 The group nodded in agreement, put on their backpacks, and headed into the woods.

10 One hour later, Team Orange was most definitely lost.

11 "Are you sure we passed this tree already?" Raoul asked, nervously.

12 Avery answered, "Yes, we made this X on it so we could tell, remember? The lake is north of the campsite, but we keep walking around like a dog chasing its tail."

13 "I have a feeling someone else is going to enjoy our 'sweet pie of victory' tonight," Maria added.

14 Lea had to get the team's spirits up if they were to make it back to camp.

15 "Did anyone bring a phone? Maybe we could text someone," Lea said.

16 "We weren't allowed to bring them, remember? The teachers want us to 'have a good time without technology,'" Sophia complained.

17 Maria dug around in her bag. "I have a water bottle, granola bars, a sewing kit, a piece of cork, and a tin pan. Oh, and some magnets. Don't ask me why."

18 Lea's eyes lit up. "There's hope! Mr. Fath's science class is going to pay off! We have everything we need!"

19 Raoul was not so sure. "Are we going to sew our way home?"

20 Avery exclaimed, "Compasses! We can make a compass to get us back to camp!"

21 Working together like busy bees on a mission, the group created a compass. Finally, the team identified north and started their journey back to camp.

22 "There you are! We were beginning to worry," Mr. Fath said as he headed their way. "You've been gone for an hour. Hate to break it to you, but your winning streak is over."

23 "That's okay, Mr. Fath. We made it back to camp thanks to Maria's backpack and your science class, which is a win in my book!" Lea smiled.

1 The simile "walking around like a dog chasing its tail" in paragraph 12 describes how the team was —

  A walking around in circles

  B walking in a straight path

  C walking up a mountain

  D walking for miles

2 What is the problem in the story?

  F Mr. Fath won Capture the Flag.

  G The children do not have their phones.

  H Team Orange is lost in the woods.

  J Raoul forgot his backpack.

3 The reader can infer that Lea —

  A easily gives up when faced with a tough problem

  B cannot live without her phone at camp

  C wishes her friends had chosen to be on another team

  D is a leader who likes science and winning games

4 Which event happens right before the team makes the compass?

  F "Last year, Lea's Team Orange won, and she was ready for a repeat performance."

  G "The lake is north of the campsite, but we keep walking around."

  H "Lea gathered Team Orange together before they headed out."

  J "Finally, the team identified north and started their journey back to camp."

Quick Tip

If you are not sure about the correct answer, try to eliminate answers that are definitely incorrect.

PLOT

COLLABORATE

The plot is the structure, or events, in a story. When you analyze a plot, you discuss the rising action, climax, falling action, and resolution. **Rising action** is the events where conflict begins to build up in the story. The **climax** is the most intense part in a story. It is the turning point. The **falling action** is where the conflict starts to get solved. The **resolution** is the solution to the problem.

Analyze the plot elements in "Compass Campward Bound." Then complete the chart below.

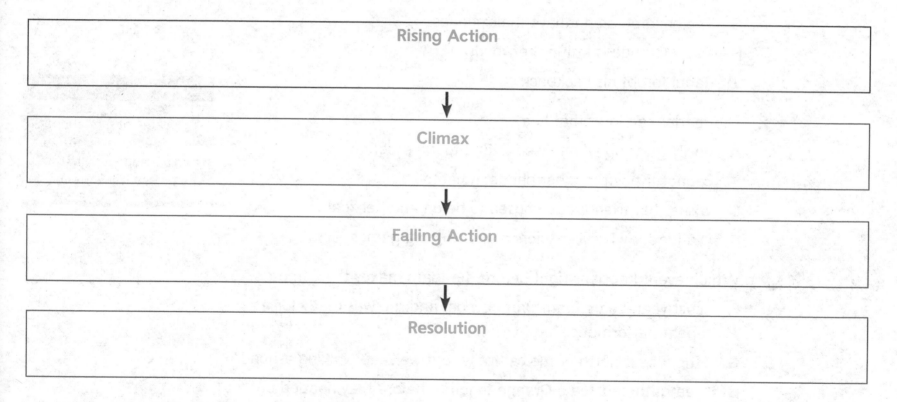

Rising Action

↓

Climax

↓

Falling Action

↓

Resolution

ANTONYMS

COLLABORATE

Two words that have opposite meanings are called **antonyms**. *Quiet* and *noisy* are antonyms. Writers use antonyms to compare and contrast ideas in their writing. You can find antonyms for words in a thesaurus.

- Choose a word from a text you have read in this unit.

- Use a print or online thesaurus to identify antonyms for the word.

Word	Antonym

PROVERBS AND ADAGES

COLLABORATE

Proverbs and **adages** are short sayings that many people believe to be true. Match the proverbs and adages with their meanings. Use the Internet to help you if necessary.

1. Curiosity killed the cat.
2. The best things in life are free.
3. Two wrongs don't make a right.
4. Practice makes perfect.

A. You cannot buy the most important things.
B. Doing something over and over again is the only way to get better.
C. Because someone behaves badly doesn't mean you have to act the same way.
D. Being nosy might get you in trouble.

CREATE A DIGITAL BROCHURE

A **brochure** tells information about a topic, an event, or a place. Make a digital brochure you can share online.

- Research an archaeological dig in your state. Tell where it is located, what archaeologists have discovered, and other important details.

- Include photographs, illustrations, maps, or diagrams of the archaeological dig. Use the template below to map out your research. Then use the template to create your brochure online.

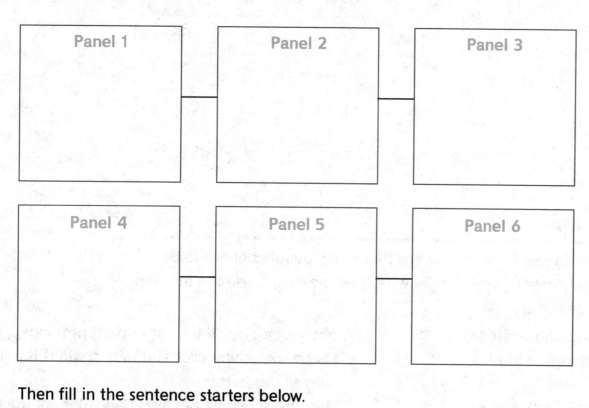

| Panel 1 | Panel 2 | Panel 3 |
| Panel 4 | Panel 5 | Panel 6 |

Then fill in the sentence starters below.

The dig I researched is _____

This dig is important because _____

CONDUCT A MAGNET EXPERIMENT

COLLABORATE

Experiments are tests that scientists conduct to answer questions. For example, what happens when you hold a magnet next to certain items? Conduct a magnet experiment and record your results.

- Gather the materials: penny or other coin, paper, aluminum foil, paper clip.

- Hold a magnet near each item.

- Record what you observe in the second column of the chart.

- Indicate whether the item is magnetic. Explain your observations.

Is It Magnetic?

Materials	Observations and Explanation
coin	
paper	
foil	
paper clip	

After you finish, discuss with your partner some other questions you have about magnets. What questions interest you the most? Why?

(t to b, l to r) revers/Shutterstock.com, (1) kyoshino/Getty Images, (2) Ken Cavanagh/McGraw-Hill Education, (3) David Toase/Getty Images, (4) Ken Cavanagh/McGraw-Hill Education

TRACK YOUR PROGRESS

WHAT DID YOU LEARN?

Use the Rubric to evaluate yourself on the skills that you learned in this unit. Write your scores in the boxes below.

4	3	2	1
I can successfully identify all examples of this skill.	I can identify most examples of this skill.	I can identify a few examples of this skill.	I need to work on this skill more.

☐ Sequence   ☐ Problem and Solution   ☐ Make Inferences

☐ Antonyms   ☐ Similes   ☐ Proverbs and Adages

☐ Author's Purpose   ☐ Plot

Something that I need to work more on is _____ because

_____

_____

_____

Text to Self Think back over the texts that you have read in this unit. Choose one text and write a short paragraph explaining a personal connection that you have made to the text.

I made a personal connection to _____ because _____

_____

_____

_____

Present Your Map

COLLABORATE

Discuss how you will present your map. Use the Presenting Checklist as you practice your presentation. Discuss the sentence starters below and write your answers.

Quick Tip

As you rehearse, plan a presentation that allows time for questions and feedback. Practice will improve your presentation and give you confidence to do the best you can.

An interesting fact that I learned about the established settlements is _____

_____

_____

I would like to know more about _____

_____

_____

✔ Presenting Checklist

☐ Rehearse your presentation in front of a friend. Ask for feedback.

☐ Speak slowly and clearly.

☐ Read the map title and map key.

☐ Point to areas of the map as you give your presentation.

☐ Check your map for any spelling or grammar mistakes.

FatCamera/E+/Getty Images

Talk About It

? **Essential Question**

How have our energy
resources changed
over the years?

The building in the photo has three wind turbines that help produce electricity. Wind energy is a renewable energy source. Oil and gas are nonrenewable energy sources. Once they are used up, they are gone forever.

Talk with a partner about what you can do to help conserve energy. In the word web below, write words you have learned about energy resources.

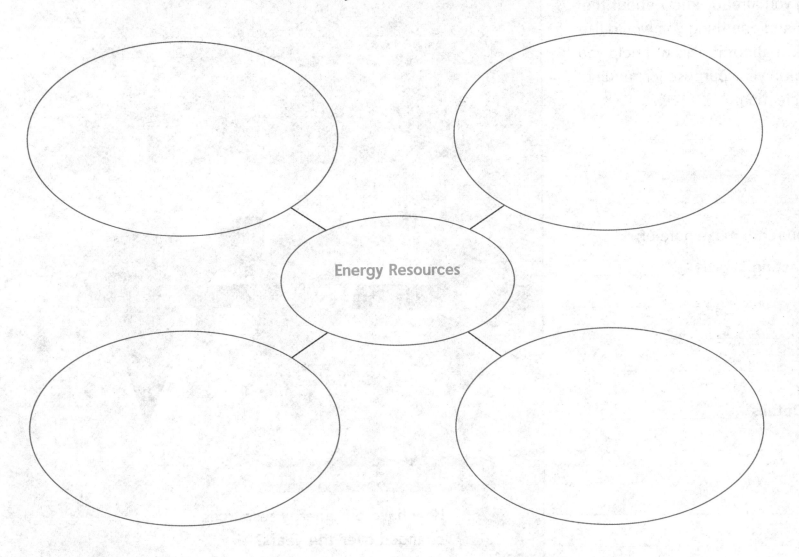

Energy Resources

 Go online to **my.mheducation.com** and read the "Fueling the Future" Blast. Think about how our resources have changed over the years. Then blast back your response.

TAKES NOTES

Read the title. Then write one thing you already know about the topic and one thing you would like to learn about it. This will help you establish your purpose for reading the selection.

_____

_____

_____

As you read, make note of:

Interesting Words _____

_____

_____

_____

Key Details _____

_____

_____

_____

_____

_____

The Great ENERGY DEBATE

Essential Question

?

How have our energy resources changed over the years?

Read about a classroom debate over energy resources.

Our energy debate will be an **incredible** event, but I need to study. Our teacher won't tell us which side of the debate we'll be on until the day before it happens, which means we'll have to preplan arguments for both sides.

The debate will be next Tuesday and will include a discussion about different energy sources. Each team will have a microphone. One team will talk about the benefits of an energy source, and the other team will talk about its drawbacks. We'll have to learn about the environmental **consequences** related to each resource, as well as the costs.

FIND TEXT EVIDENCE

Read

Paragraph 1
Latin Prefixes

Find the word that means "to prepare before." **Circle** the prefix of the word.

Paragraph 2
Main Idea and Key Details

Draw a box around the main idea of the debate. Write it here.

_____

_____

Underline two key details about the debate.

Reread

Author's Craft

What words does the author use to help you understand the main idea of the second paragraph?

(bkgd) Echo/Cultura/Getty Images; (t) Reggie Casagrande/Photographer's Choice RF/Getty Images (b) Erik Isakson/Blend Images/Getty Images

FIND TEXT EVIDENCE

Read

Paragraphs 1–2

Greek Prefixes

The prefix *geo-* means "earth." **Underline** the word that has this prefix. Look up the meaning of the word and write it here.

_____

_____

Ask and Answer Questions

Circle the answer to the question, "What will happen if we keep using fossil fuels at the same rate?"

Sidebar

Look at the sidebar. **Draw a box** around the sentence that identifies which resources are used to produce energy.

Reread

Author's Craft

What details does the author present about the future of fossil fuels as an energy source?

What Is Energy?

Energy is the ability to do work or make a change. It also is a source of power for making electricity or doing mechanical work. We use the wind, the sun, fossil fuels, and biofuels to produce energy. Burning coal produces heat energy that is converted into electrical energy. We use that energy to light our houses. Solar energy comes from the sun. Solar panels convert sunlight into electrical energy.

We may be asked to debate the future of gasoline as an energy source. If so, I would say that gasoline is made from oil, a fossil fuel. According to geologists, fossil fuels formed over hundreds of millions of years from ancient plant and animal remains. But here's the problem: we use these fuels far faster than it takes them to form. Because fossil fuels are nonrenewable resources, if we keep using them, eventually there will be none left. Plus burning these fuels pollutes the air!

It is easy to be hypercritical of fossil fuels. However, most of our cars and factories use this type of fuel, and therefore changing everything would be a huge undertaking.

If we are asked to debate the use of wind energy, we would have to know that this is a **renewable** energy source. For example, unlike fossil fuels, wind will never run out. One large wind turbine could produce enough energy for a whole city! In addition, this method doesn't damage the environment. Turbines can be placed all over the world to capture wind energy. Then the energy from the turbines is **converted** into electrical energy. But there is a drawback. Wind may not be as **efficient** as other energy sources. Only about 30 or 40 percent of all wind energy is changed into electricity. It would be very expensive to have wind turbines **installed** all over the world.

This debate is important for people in the United States. Our country makes up only about 5 percent of the entire world's population. Yet we **consume** about 30 percent of the world's energy. It is not a **coincidence** that students are asked to take part in these debates. We will probably have to make these decisions when we are adults. The debate will be difficult, but I will be ready!

Summarize

Use your notes and the photos to orally summarize the key details in "The Great Energy Debate."

NARRATIVE NONFICTION

FIND TEXT EVIDENCE

Read

Paragraphs 1–2

Main Idea and Key Details

Underline at least two key details about wind energy.

Ask and Answer Questions

Write a question you would ask at the debate.

_____

_____

Reread

Author's Craft

How does the author show you that the narrator will be ready for the debate?

Fluency

With a partner, read aloud the first paragraph on page 103. Make sure you speak clearly and at a steady speed. This will help you read accurately.

(bkgd) Echo/Cultura/Getty Images; (br) Hal Bergman/Photodisc/Getty Images; (bl) Livio Sinibaldi/Digital Vision/Getty Images

Vocabulary

Use the example sentences to talk with a partner about each word. Then answer the questions.

coincidence

It was a **coincidence** that both Eric and Tarik were at the store yesterday.

What kind of coincidence have you experienced?

_____

_____

consequences

The **consequences** of too much rain can be flooded roads.

What are some consequences of not doing your homework?

_____

_____

consume

Small cars **consume** less fuel than large trucks.

What do people consume?

_____

_____

converted

We **converted** the classroom into a science lab.

What is a synonym for *converted*?

_____

_____

efficient

The **efficient** plumber got the job done quickly and easily.

What is an efficient way for you to get to school?

_____

_____

 Build Your Word List Pick an interesting word that you noted on page 100. Look up the meaning of the word in a print or digital dictionary. Then write a sentence using the word.

incredible

We saw an **incredible** thunderstorm.

What have you seen that is incredible?

_____

_____

installed

The town **installed** a new monument in the park.

What is a synonym for _installed_?

_____

_____

renewable

When my library card expired, the librarian told me it was **renewable**.

What is something that is not renewable?

_____

_____

Latin and Greek Prefixes

A **prefix** is a word part added to the front of a word to change its meaning. Some prefixes come from Latin, such as:

non- = not   _pre-_ = before

Other prefixes come from Greek, such as:

hyper- = excessively   _bio-_ = life

🔍 FIND TEXT EVIDENCE

In "The Great Energy Debate," I see the word biofuels _on page 102. Bio- is a Greek prefix that means "life." So_ biofuels _are fuels made from living things._

We use the wind, the sun, fossil fuels, and biofuels to produce energy.

Your Turn Use your knowledge of prefixes and context clues to find the meanings of the following words in "The Great Energy Debate."

nonrenewable, _page 102_ _____

_____

hypercritical, _page 102_ _____

_____

Livio Snibaldi/Digital Vision/Getty Images

Ask and Answer Questions

When you read an informational text, you may come across new information. Asking questions about the text and reading to find the answer can help you understand new information. As you reread "The Great Energy Debate," ask and answer questions about the text.

🔍 **FIND TEXT EVIDENCE**

When you first read "The Great Energy Debate," you may have asked yourself why the narrator said on page 101 that the students had to "preplan arguments for both sides."

Quick Tip

Make a list of questions you have about the text before, during, and after reading. As you reread, some of your questions may be answered. If not, discuss those questions with your partner or teacher. This will help you better understand the text and gain more information.

Page 101

> Our energy debate will be an incredible event, but I need to study. Our teacher won't tell us which side of the debate we'll be on until the day before it happens, which means we'll have to preplan arguments for both sides.

The text says the teacher wouldn't tell which side of the issue students would be debating. I wonder how the students will get ready for the debate. The narrator says that they will have to preplan arguments for both sides. This is the answer to my question.

Your Turn Reread "The Great Energy Debate" to ask and answer questions of your own using the Ask and Answer Questions strategy.

_____

_____

_____

Sidebars

The selection "The Great Energy Debate" is narrative nonfiction. A narrative nonfiction

- tells a story
- presents facts and information about a topic
- uses a text structure to organize information
- includes text features, such as sidebars

 FIND TEXT EVIDENCE

I can tell that "The Great Energy Debate" is narrative nonfiction. It tells a story about students preparing for a debate while providing facts about energy sources. It also has text features, such as a sidebar.

Page 102

What Is Energy?

Energy is the ability to do work or make a change. It also is a source of power for making electricity or doing mechanical work. We use the wind, the sun, fossil fuels, and biofuels to produce energy. Burning coal produces heat energy that is converted into electrical energy. We use that energy to light our houses. Solar energy comes from the sun. Solar panels convert sunlight into electrical energy.

We may be asked to debate the future of gasoline as an energy source. If so, I would say that gasoline is made from oil, a fossil fuel. According to geologists, fossil fuels formed over hundreds of millions of years from ancient plant and animal remains. But here's the problem: we use these fuels far faster than it takes them to form. Because fossil fuels are nonrenewable resources, if we keep using them, eventually there will be none left. Plus burning these fuels pollutes the air!

It is easy to be hypercritical of fossil fuels. However, most of our cars and factories use this type of fuel, and therefore changing everything would be a huge undertaking.

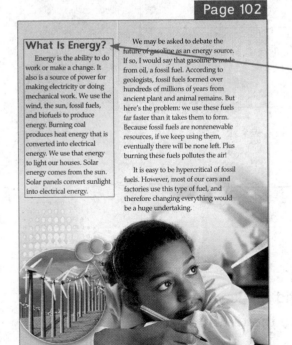

Readers to Writers

Writers use sidebars to include additional information. The extra information should relate to the topic of the article. Sometimes photographs, illustrations, maps, or diagrams are included in a sidebar. How can you use sidebars in your own writing?

Sidebars

Sidebars provide more information to help explain the topic. Sidebars are read after the main part of the text.

 Your Turn Find and reread the sidebar in "The Great Energy Debate." Explain what you learned from it. How is this additional information helpful?

_____

_____

_____

Main Idea and Key Details

The main idea is the most important idea or point that an author makes in a paragraph or section of text. Key details give important information to support the main idea.

FIND TEXT EVIDENCE

When I reread the first paragraph of "The Great Energy Debate" on page 102, I can identify the key details about fossil fuels. Next, I can think about what those details have in common. This text evidence helps me figure out the main idea of the selection.

Quick Tip

To help you find the main idea, think about the question, "What is this paragraph mostly about?"

Then look for key details that tell about the main idea.

Main Idea
If we keep using fossil fuels, eventually there will be none left.

Detail
Fossil fuels take hundreds of millions of years to form.

Detail
We use fossil fuels faster than it takes them to form.

Detail
Fossil fuels are nonrenewable resources.

Your Turn Reread the first paragraph on page 103. Find the key details and list them in the graphic organizer on page 109. Use the details to determine the main idea.

Main Idea

Detail

Detail

Detail

Respond to Reading

COLLABORATE

Discuss the prompt below. Think about how the author presents information about different sources of energy. Use your notes and graphic organizer.

How does the author organize the information about renewable and nonrenewable energy sources?

_____

_____

_____

_____

_____

_____

_____

_____

_____

_____

_____

_____

Quick Tip

Use these sentence starters to discuss the different energy sources.

- *The author organizes the text to tell about . . .*

- *Benefits and drawbacks of renewable energy sources are . . .*

- *Benefits and drawbacks of nonrenewable energy sources are . . .*

Grammar Connections

As you write your response, you can look back through the text to check the spelling of complex words. Pay attention to words with prefixes or suffixes, such as *nonrenewable* and *environment*.

Key Word Search

Key words help you search for information in a search engine. Key words are the most important words related to a subject.

- To find out more about wind energy and how much it costs, some key words to use are *wind energy*.
- Narrow the search to get more useful information. Put in quotation marks words that go together, and add search terms such as AND, OR, and NOT.

> "wind energy" AND costs
> "wind energy" OR "renewable energy" AND Texas

What other key words could you add to this search?

_____

_____

Design a Game or Puzzle With a partner or in a group, make a game or crossword puzzle about energy resources.

- Think about what you know about renewable and nonrenewable resources and what you want to learn more about.
- Make a list of key words to use as search terms.
- Use a search engine to find your information.
- Highlight the most interesting facts.

Build your game or crossword puzzle around the facts you gather. Write directions for your game or crossword. Take turns restating the directions to make sure that they make sense. After you finish, you will share your work with the class.

Tech Tip

You can find crossword and other puzzle generators online. They can help you design a puzzle. What key words will you use to find them?

1:26 PM

Q "renewable energy"

"renewable energy" ×

ALL   NEWS   IMAGES   VIDEOS   MAPS

Renewable Energy

Renewable energy comes from renewable resources. Some examples of renewable resources are the sun, the wind, ocean tides, and geothermal heat. These resources are replaced quickly in nature.

GreenLandStudio/Shutterstock.com, (inset) SasPartout/age fotostock

Energy Island

Literature Anthology:
pages 458–475

? **Why does the author emphasize the word *ordinary* when describing the island of Samsø?**

Talk About It Reread **Literature Anthology** page 460. Turn to your partner and discuss what the author tells you about the island of Samsø.

Cite Text Evidence What does the author describe as ordinary? Write text evidence in the web below.

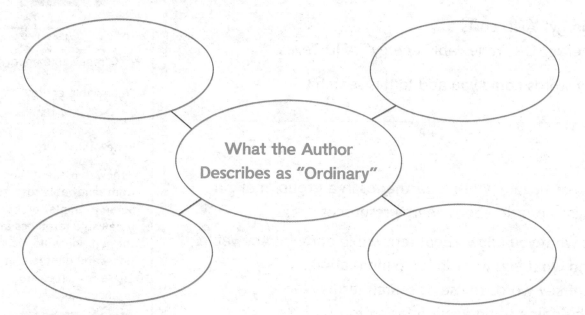

What the Author
Describes as "Ordinary"

 Make Inferences

The narrator says that in the winter, families play games inside and use heaters to keep warm. What can you infer about the winter weather in Samsø?

Quick Tip

After you finish reading a page, ask yourself a question about what you just read. Then reread to find the answer to the question.

Write The author emphasizes the word *ordinary* when describing the island of Samsø to _____

_____

_____

How is the author's use of the phrase "hold on to your hats" important to the idea for Samsø's energy independence?

Talk About It Reread page 463. Turn to your partner and talk about the idea Kathrine suggests for the island. Based on her suggestion, why would the residents of Samsø need to hold on to their hats?

Cite Text Evidence Explain the two meanings of "hold on to your hats" as they relate to the story. Write text evidence in the chart below.

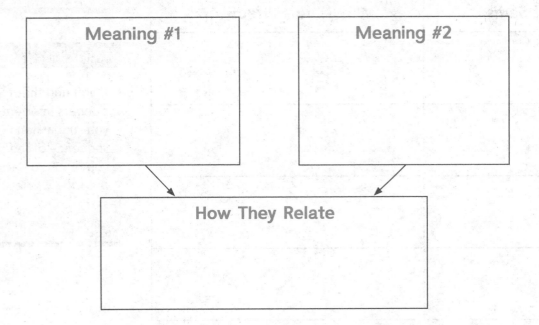

Meaning #1	Meaning #2

How They Relate

Write The author's use of the phrase "hold on to your hats" is important to the idea for Samsø's energy independence because _____

_____

_____

_____

Synthesize Information

Think about experiences you have had on a windy day. What do they tell you about the power of wind? Combine what you know about wind with what you find out in the text to create a new understanding. Do you think wind power would be a good energy source where you live? Why or why not?

Quick Tip

Use these sentence starters when you talk about Kathrine's idea.

- *Kathrine suggests using this kind of energy because . . .*

- *The residents should hold on to their hats because . . .*

Why does the author want you to picture an active, enthusiastic island at the end of the selection?

Talk About It Reread page 472 of the **Literature Anthology.** Turn to your partner and discuss how the island of Samsø has changed.

Cite Text Evidence How does the author's word choice show enthusiasm for the changes on the island? Write text evidence in the chart below.

Description of Samsø	Why Is This Effective?

Write The author wants you to picture an active, enthusiastic island at the end of the selection to _____

_____

_____

Evaluate Information

Sidebars give information that helps you better understand the main text. What did you learn about wind energy from the sidebar on page 471? Tell how it helped you better understand the story.

Quick Tip

If you find that the sidebars interfere with your understanding of the sequence of the story as you read, go back and read the whole story from start to finish. Then read each sidebar at the end.

Respond to Reading

Discuss the prompt below. Apply your own knowledge of energy sources to inform your answer. Use your notes and graphic organizer.

How does the author organize the text and use text features to tell you about wind energy and the people of Energy Island?

_____

_____

_____

_____

_____

_____

_____

_____

_____

_____

_____

Quick Tip

Use these sentence starters to organize your text evidence.

- In the beginning, the author describes Samsø as . . .

- In the middle of the selection, the author shows . . .

- At the end of the selection, the author points out how . . .

Self-Selected Reading

Choose a text. Read the first two pages. If five or more words are unfamiliar, pick another text. Fill in your writer's notebook with the title, author, genre, and your purpose for reading.

RimDream/Shutterstock.com

Of Fire and Water

Literature Anthology:
pages 478–481

The Gift of Fire

[1] To appease the angry Zeus, humans offered him abundant sacrifices. They kept little for themselves.

[2] Prometheus thought this was wrong. He tricked Zeus into choosing a cleverly disguised sacrificial dish rather than a richer dish for his offering. The dish Zeus chose looked delicious on the outside, but within it consisted entirely of fat and bones. When Zeus realized the trick, he took fire away from humans.

[3] Prometheus pleaded with Zeus to change his mind, but Zeus forbade him to bring fire to humans. Prometheus watched his creations eat raw meat and shiver in the cold and dark. Finally, he went to Athena for help, and she led Prometheus to a hidden entrance to Mount Olympus where he could capture fire for humans.

Reread paragraphs 1 to 3 and use the prompts to take notes in the text. **Underline** two examples in paragraph 3 that show what happened to humans when fire was taken from them. Write them here.

 1 _____

 2 _____

COLLABORATE

Talk with a partner about how the author shows the importance of fire. **Circle** text evidence in paragraph 3 that shows what Prometheus felt the need to do. How does the title fit the myth's message? Use your annotations to support your response.

_____

_____

_____

1996 PhotoDisc, Inc./Getty Images

Water vs. Wisdom

[1] Poseidon was the first to offer a gift. Raising his trident high over his head, he struck the rocky hill with a powerful blow. Cecrops watched in amazement as the hole filled with water. In the hot, dry land of Greece, water was a precious resource.

[2] The people of Attica were impressed. They seemed ready to rule in favor of Poseidon until Athena told Cecrops to taste the water. A servant brought a cup to the king, who drank it and spit it out. It was salt water! There was no use for that in Attica.

[3] Then, Athena came forward with the branch of a tree that no human had seen before. She planted the branch in the ground, and an olive tree sprang up in its place. The king nodded, pleased. His people now had a source of food, wood, and oil.

Reread paragraph 1. **Circle** the words the author uses to emphasize the importance of water to the people of Attica. Write those words here.

_____

COLLABORATE

Reread paragraphs 2 and 3. Talk about how the author compares Poseidon's and Athena's gifts to the people of Attica. If water was such an important resource to the people of Attica, why do they choose Athena's gift?

_____

_____

_____

Why is "Water vs. Wisdom" a good title for this myth? Use your annotations to support your response.

_____

_____

_____

_____

Photodisc/Getty Images

? **What does the author suggest about resources in both myths?**

COLLABORATE

Talk About It Reread the paragraphs on pages 116 and 117. With a partner, compare and contrast the information in these two myths. What does the author want you to understand about resources?

Cite Text Evidence Compare and contrast what the myths suggest about resources. Write text evidence in the graphic organizer below.

Evaluate Information

As you reread, think about which words and ideas the texts have in common. Then think about the words and ideas that are different in the two texts. Use this information to figure out the authors' message.

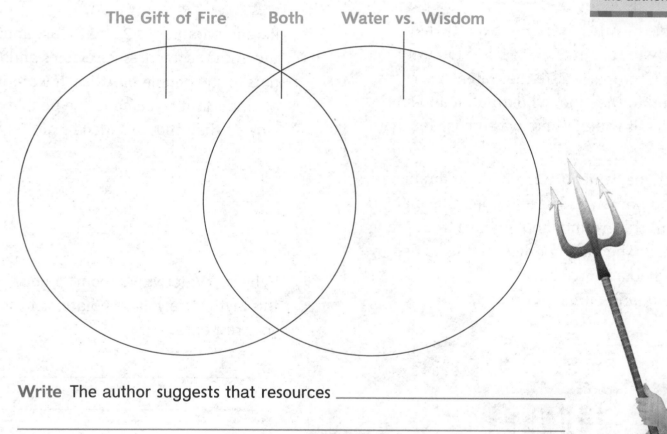

The Gift of Fire   Both   Water vs. Wisdom

Write The author suggests that resources _____

_____

Elements of a Myth

Myths are stories from ancient cultures around the world that have many elements in common. For example, myths often include the intervention of gods or goddesses. They may offer explanations for natural occurrences, such as lightning. Myths teach a lesson about right and wrong.

FIND TEXT EVIDENCE

On page 479, in paragraphs 2 and 3 of "Of Fire and Water," the narrator tells what happened to humans after Zeus took fire away and how Prometheus got it back. The author tells about the importance of fire to the ancient people and creates an extraordinary event to get fire back.

> As the chariot of the sun god Helios passed by, Prometheus stole a spark and hid it inside a fennel stalk.

Your Turn Reread page 117.

- What gift does Poseidon give Cecrops?

  _____

  _____

- How does this explain something in the natural world?

  _____

Quick Tip

When looking for answers to questions, read the question and then reread the text. Underline evidence that will help you answer the question.

Text Connections

? **How does the artist focus your attention on the resources in the painting? How is this similar to the way that the authors of the *Energy Island,* "Of Fire and Water," and "Fueling the Future" Blast help you understand the importance of natural resources?**

Quick Tip

Study the painting. First, look at the things that take up most of the space in the painting. Then look at the things in the background. This will help you compare the painting to the texts you have read.

Talk About It With a partner, look at the painting and read the caption. Talk about the natural resources you see and how some of them are being used.

Cite Text Evidence **Circle** clues in the painting and caption that show how natural resources are being used. **Draw a line** to separate the sky and the land. Notice how the artist composed the painting so your eye is drawn to the windmill. Now think about how the authors of this week's selections use words and phrases to help you see the importance of natural resources.

Write The artist and authors help me understand how important natural resources are by _____

_____

_____

_____

_____

_____

This oil painting is called *The Windmill at Wijk bij Duurstede.* It was painted by a Dutch artist named Jacob van Ruisdael between 1668 and 1670.

Rijksmuseum, Amsterdam

Present Your Work

COLLABORATE

Discuss how you will present your game or crossword puzzle to the class. Decide how you will explain the rules and encourage your classmates to participate. Use the presenting checklist as you practice your presentation. Discuss the sentence starters below and write your answers.

SCIENCE

Quick Tip

Before sharing your game or puzzle, prepare a short explanation of your key word search. Tell your classmates how you used key words to research your topic.

Presenting Checklist

☐ Practice presenting the rules of the game or puzzle in front of a friend. Ask for feedback.

☐ Speak clearly at an understandable volume and pace, and stop to ask if listeners understand the rules as you present them.

☐ Use an energetic tone to encourage your classmates to play the game or solve the puzzle.

☐ Write a few facts from the game or puzzle on an index card so you are prepared for questions.

☐ Listen carefully to questions from the audience.

An interesting fact I learned about energy resources is _____

_____

_____

I would like to know more about _____

_____

_____

Diane Diederich/Getty Images

Literature Anthology:
pages 458-475

Expert Model

Features of Narrative Nonfiction

Narrative nonfiction gives facts about real people and events.
Narrative nonfiction

- tells a factual story in an interesting way

- provides facts and specific details about a topic

- often includes text features, such as sidebars

Analyze an Expert Model Studying narrative nonfiction will help you
learn how to write a narrative nonfiction essay. **Reread** page 459 of
Energy Island in the **Literature Anthology**. Write your answers below.

How does the author's use of informal language help make the narrative

interesting? _____

_____

_____

Reread the last two paragraphs. What inference can you make about the

text structure of the narrative? _____

_____

_____

_____

Word Wise

The author uses the
pronouns *we, us, our,* and
ourselves. He is using the
first-person plural
pronouns to narrate. By
using the first person, the
author makes it feel as if
the whole community is
sharing its experience
with the reader.

Plan: Choose Your Topic

Brainstorm With a partner, brainstorm all the different natural resources that you use during a typical day. For example, you use water when you take a shower. You use electricity when you turn on lights. List some of the natural resources you use below.

_____

_____

_____

Quick Tip

To help you plan your writing, ask yourself:

- *What do I want my audience to learn?*

- *Where can I find facts and details about my topic?*

- *What text features can I use to help my readers understand key points?*

Writing Prompt Think about why conserving resources helps society. What can you do to use less water, less electricity, less gas? Write a narrative nonfiction essay explaining what you could do to conserve natural resources.

Purpose and Audience An **author's purpose** is his or her main reason for writing. When writing narrative nonfiction, the purpose is to inform and entertain.

Think about the intended audience for your essay. Who will read it?

My audience will be _____

I will use _____ language when I write my essay.

Plan In your writer's notebook, use a concept web to map your ideas on how to conserve resources. Put "I can conserve natural resources by . . ." in the center oval. Then write your ideas in the smaller circles.

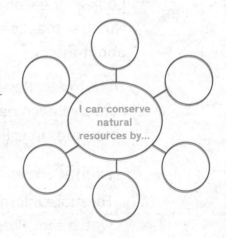

I can conserve natural resources by...

Plan: Sequence

Putting Events in Order In a narrative, writers usually tell about events in the order in which they happen. This sequence of events helps readers understand what happened and why it happened. Writers use sequence words and phrases to signal the order of events. Sequence words include *first, later, next, then,* and *finally.*

Read the paragraph below. Circle the sequence words that signal the order of events.

> To make a peanut butter and jelly sandwich, I first get out two slices of bread. Then I open the jar of peanut butter and the jar of jelly. Next, I spread peanut butter on one piece of bread and jelly on the other. Finally, I put both pieces of bread together.

Look at the web you made in your writer's notebook. Number the ideas in the order in which you want to write about them.

Take Notes Research information and ideas on how to conserve each natural resource in your concept web. Write your notes in your writer's notebook.

Digital Tools

For more information on writing narrative nonfiction, watch the "Purpose of Informational Writing" tutorial. Go to **my.mheducation.com**.

---

wavebreakmedia/Shutterstock.com

Draft

Specific Details Authors of narrative nonfiction use facts, details, examples, and statistics to give readers evidence about the topic. In the example below, the writer explains how much of our energy comes from waterpower. The writer states the main idea in the first sentence and includes specific details to support the main idea.

Grammar Connection

Do not start a sentence with a number. For example, do not write *7.8 percent of the power made in the United States is from hydropower.* Instead rewrite it to state: *In the United States, 7.8 percent of the power made is from hydropower.*

> I went to the library to find out how much of our energy comes from waterpower. I discovered that about 7.8 percent of the power made in the United States is from hydropower. To my disbelief, a large amount comes from fossil fuels and nuclear power, too. I had hoped to see higher numbers for renewable resources.

Use the above paragraph as a model to write about one way to conserve a natural resource. In the first sentence, give a statistic related to the resource.

_____

_____

_____

_____

_____

Write a Draft Use your concept web and notes to help you write your first draft in your writer's notebook. Make sure that for every idea you write about, you include a few facts as evidence.

Revise

Quick Tip

Linking Words Writers use linking words, such as *in addition, also, for example, though, however,* and *therefore,* to connect ideas. Read the paragraph below. Then revise it by adding linking words, so the transition between ideas is smooth.

As you revise, make sure the events are in the correct order. Then you can connect ideas with linking words or phrases.

> There are a number of problems with using fossil fuels to make gasoline. Fossil fuels are a nonrenewable resource. They pollute the air. It is better to make cars that do not use too much gasoline.

Revision As you revise your draft, you can improve your sentences by combining and rearranging ideas to make your sentences clearer and easier to read. Also, check that you also have enough specific facts, quotes, and statistics related to your topic.

sripfoto/Shutterstock.com

Peer Conferences

COLLABORATE

Review a Draft Listen carefully as a partner reads his or her work aloud. Take notes about what you like and what is difficult to follow. Make a list of questions you have about the topic that are unclear to you. Make suggestions you think will make the writing stronger. Use these sentence starters.

I like the beginning of your essay because . . .

I think you could use a fact to support . . .

I wonder if you could add a linking word . . .

I'm not sure I understand what happened after . . .

Partner Feedback After your partner gives you feedback on your draft, write one of the suggestions that you will use in your revision. Refer to the rubric on page 129 as you give feedback.

Based on my partner's feedback, I will _____

_____

_____

_____

After you finish giving each other feedback, reflect on the peer conference. What was helpful? What might you do differently next time?

Revision As you revise your draft, use the Revising Checklist to help you figure out what text you may need to add, combine, rearrange, or delete. Remember to use the rubric on page 129 to help with your revision.

> ✓ **Revising Checklist**
>
> ☐ Is my essay in the correct sequence, with a clear beginning, middle, and end?
>
> ☐ Do I include enough facts and specific details to explain my topic?
>
> ☐ Do I use good linking words to show the connections between ideas?
>
> ☐ Do I help my audience understand my topic?

Edit and Proofread

When you **edit** and **proofread** your writing, you look for and correct mistakes in spelling, punctuation, capitalization, and grammar. Reading through a revised draft multiple times can help you make sure you're catching any errors. Use the checklist below to edit your sentences.

Quick Tip

When proofreading, look for one type of problem at a time. Concentrate on spelling the first time you proofread your work. Then go back and look at sentence structure and grammar. Finally, read it to check punctuation.

✔ Editing Checklist

- ☐ Are singular and plural pronouns used correctly?
- ☐ Do quotes from any primary sources have quotation marks?
- ☐ Are there any run-on sentences or sentence fragments?
- ☐ Do your sentences have the correct subject-verb agreement?
- ☐ Are there specific details to support the essay?
- ☐ Is there a logical order to my essay?

List two mistakes you found as you proofread your essay.

1 _____

_____

2 _____

_____

Publish, Present, and Evaluate

Publishing When you **publish** your writing, you create a clean, neat final copy that is free of mistakes. Adding visuals can make your writing more interesting. Consider including illustrations, photos, or maps to help make your essay more interesting.

Presentation When you are ready to **present** your work, rehearse your presentation. Use the Presenting Checklist to help you.

Evaluate After you publish your writing, use the rubric below to **evaluate** your writing.

What did you do successfully? _____

What needs more work? _____

✓ **Presenting Checklist**

☐ Look at the audience.

☐ Speak slowly and clearly.

☐ Speak loud enough so that everyone can hear you.

☐ Answer questions thoughtfully, using details about the topic.

4	3	2	1
• writing follows a logical sequence with a strong beginning, middle, and end • writing is supported by facts and other specific details • linking words are used to organize ideas and create strong transitions	• writing has a satisfactory structure, with a beginning, middle, and end • writing has some facts and specific details related to the topic • a few linking words are used to connect ideas	• the sequence of the story is evident but hard to follow • there are few facts and specific details related to the topic • a few ideas are connected with linking words, but there are other parts that could use better transitions	• does not have an identifiable sequence • there are almost no facts and specific details related to the topic • ideas are not connected with linking words

COLLABORATE

Stories, music, and dance are all part of a person's cultural tradition and history. Cultures preserve traditions by passing them on to the next generation. This helps connect the present to the past.

What are some traditions that you enjoy? Write words that describe them. Then talk to your partner about how traditions connect people.

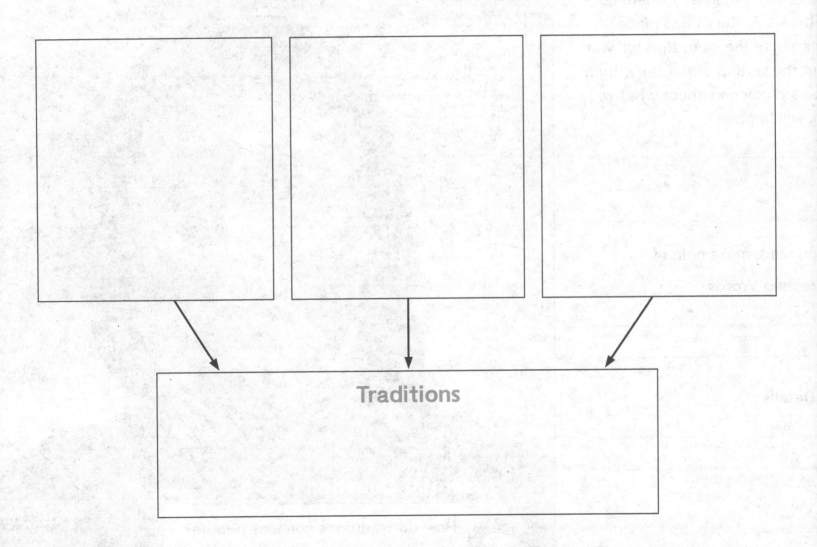

Traditions

Go online to **my.mheducation.com** and read the "Living Your Past" Blast. Think about how family traditions and culture are passed on. Then blast back your response.

Gunter Marx/NA/Alamy Stock Photo

TAKE NOTES

Read the title and look at the illustrations. When and where do you think this story takes place? Write about the clues that tell you about the setting of the story, then make a prediction about what you think will happen.

_____

_____

_____

As you read, make note of:

Interesting Words _____

_____

_____

Key Details _____

_____

_____

_____

_____

_____

_____

A Surprise Reunion

Essential Question

How do traditions connect people?

Read how a brother and sister are reunited after many years apart.

Chief Cameahwait looked with **intensity** across the Shoshone camp. The tribe prepared for the Rabbit Dance as warriors put on their ceremonial clothes. The dance was done to **honor** the rabbit as a source of food and warm clothing. The Shoshone had used traditions such as this dance since the beginning of time to mark special occasions and remember their **ancestors**.

In the distance laughing children were playing with a ball made from rawhide. They rolled the ball into a circle drawn in the dust. If the ball rolled outside the circle, the child must **forfeit** his or her turn. Cameahwait smiled as he remembered the games he had played as a child.

But Cameahwait grimaced beneath his smile. He felt a dull pain in his stomach for his little sister. She had been snatched from the camp during a raid long ago. He **despised** those who had taken her. He closed his eyes and pictured the games they had played together. She had been scrawny, sure-footed, and had an **irritating** habit of following him everywhere, he remembered. He missed her humorous insights and her constant questions. What had become of her?

FIND TEXT EVIDENCE 🔍

Read

Paragraphs 1–3
Connotation

Underline the sentence in paragraph 3 that helps you understand the connotation of the word *grimaced.* Write the word's meaning below.

_____

_____

Theme

Circle the question Chief Cameahwait asks himself that tells you about the theme of the story.

Reread
Author's Craft

What details does the author include to help you understand how Chief Cameahwait feels about his little sister?

SHARED READ

FIND TEXT EVIDENCE

Read

Paragraphs 1–3

Dialogue

Underline the dialogue in paragraph 1 that brings Cameahwait's thoughts back to the present.

Paragraphs 4–5

Theme

Draw a box around the words in paragraph 4 that show what Captain Clark wants to talk about. How can Cameahwait help Lewis and Clark?

_____

_____

_____

_____

Reread

Author's Craft

How does knowing Cameahwait's thoughts help you predict what might happen next?

"It is time to ride," Hawk-That-Soars said, interrupting his thoughts. Cameahwait came back to reality, turned, and mounted his horse.

A man named Captain Lewis had approached the Shoshone days before. Cameahwait knew that Lewis had come in peace, and so he welcomed him and his party. Lewis told the Shoshone his story. He explained that he was part of a company with a mission: he was to explore the land that stretched from the Missouri River to the great ocean. He then asked the chief for a favor. He explained that the rest of his party was waiting at the river with a supply boat. Lewis needed the strength and **endurance** of the Shoshone horses to help transport the supplies across the difficult land. In return Lewis offered the Shoshone food and other goods.

Cameahwait's party arrived at Lewis's camp. There he met Captain Clark.

"Let's sit and discuss how we may help each other," said Clark. He led the men inside a large tent. Buffalo blankets were spread all around. As they settled inside, Lewis addressed the chief. "We travel with a woman who knows your language."

A slender woman with long, dark braids entered the tent. Her eyes adjusted to the dim light filtered through the thick cloth. She nodded to the chief. "I am Sacagawea," she said.

Cameahwait could not believe his eyes! He examined the features of her face. He watched as her expression slowly changed. He immediately knew this was the same sweet face of his lost sister.

Sacagawea quickly ran to him. Tears filled her dark eyes. The pain and sadness that Cameahwait had carried over the years **retreated** to a forgotten place.

"My brother!" she cried. "Is it really you? How long has it been?"

Lewis and Clark were happy to have been unwitting partners in this reunion. Chief Cameahwait promised them he would provide whatever help and resources they needed.

"You have given me a great gift," Cameahwait told them. "You have reunited me with my beloved sister. Our people will sing and tell stories so that all may remember and honor this day for generations to come."

Summarize

Use your notes and the images to help you summarize "A Surprise Reunion." Talk about whether your prediction on page 132 was confirmed.

FIND TEXT EVIDENCE

Read

Paragraphs 1-2
Reread

Circle the words in paragraph 2 that help you understand how Cameahwait felt about losing his sister.

Paragraphs 3-5
Theme

Underline the sentence in paragraph 5 that tells you why the Shoshone will honor that day.

Reread

Author's Craft

How does the historical setting of the story influence the events of the plot?

Fluency

Take turns reading the first paragraph on this page to a partner. Use a print or online dictionary to check that you are pronouncing words accurately.

Vocabulary

Use the example sentences to talk with a partner about each word. Then answer the questions.

ancestors

My grandmother showed me a picture of my great-grandparents and other **ancestors**.

What do you know about some of your ancestors?

_____

_____

_____

despised

Tony liked most fruits and vegetables, but he **despised** carrots.

What is an antonym for _despised?_

_____

endurance

The runners had the strength and **endurance** to finish the marathon race.

Why is it important for a marathon runner to have endurance?

_____

_____

forfeit

The team had to **forfeit** the game when two players failed to show up.

What is a synonym for _forfeit?_

_____

honor

One way we **honor** our flag and country is to say the Pledge of Allegiance.

What are some ways that you honor your parents?

_____

_____

_____

 Build Your Word List Reread the second paragraph on page 134. In your writer's notebook, write the words that help you understand the meaning of _transport_. Describe things that trucks transport.

intensity

The lion roared loudly and with great **intensity**.

Describe a time when you did something with intensity.

_____

_____

_____

irritating

Sofia found the loud buzzing of the alarm very **irritating**.

What are some things that you might describe as irritating?

_____

_____

_____

retreated

The turtle **retreated** back into its shell when it sensed danger.

What is an antonym for *retreated*?

_____

Connotation and Denotation

Connotation is an idea or feeling attached to a word. **Denotation** is the literal, dictionary definition of a word.

🔍 FIND TEXT EVIDENCE

When I read the word scrawny *on page 133 in "A Surprise Reunion," I know its connotation differs from its denotation. The connotation is "weak and vulnerable." The denotation is "very thin."*

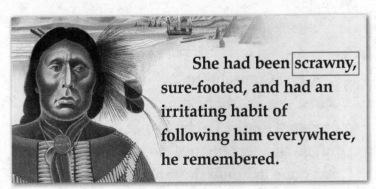

She had been scrawny, sure-footed, and had an irritating habit of following him everywhere, he remembered.

Your Turn Identify the connotation and denotation of the following words from "A Surprise Reunion."

snatched, page 133 _____

_____

slender, page 134 _____

_____

Reread

When you read historical fiction, you may come across new information or unfamiliar ideas. As you read "A Surprise Reunion," stop and reread any difficult sections of the text to make sure you understand them and remember key details.

 FIND TEXT EVIDENCE

You may not be sure what a Rabbit Dance is or why it is part of the Shoshone culture. Reread the first paragraph of "A Surprise Reunion" on page 133.

Page 133

Chief Cameahwait looked with **intensity** across the Shoshone camp. The tribe prepared for the Rabbit Dance as warriors put on their ceremonial clothes. The dance was done to **honor** the rabbit as a source of food and warm clothing. The Shoshone had used traditions such as this dance since the beginning of time to mark special occasions and remember their **ancestors**.

I read that the Rabbit Dance is a Shoshone tradition that honors the rabbit as an important food source. I can infer from this that the Shoshone have a close connection to nature.

 Your Turn What do Lewis and Clark need from Chief Cameahwait? Reread page 134 of "A Surprise Reunion" to find out. As you read, remember to use the strategy Reread to help you find the answer.

Quick Tip

When a lot of facts or ideas are presented in a text, underline the important information. Use different colored markers to keep track of the different topics.

 Evaluating Information

To help you understand and evaluate the key details of a work of historical fiction, analyze its plot elements—the story's beginning, middle, and end. During the rising action, the character identifies a problem. At the climax, the story reaches a turning point. During the falling action, the problem starts to get solved. That leads to the resolution, when the problem is solved. Talk with a partner to clarify any questions either of you may have about "A Surprise Reunion."

Dialogue

"A Surprise Reunion" is historical fiction. Historical fiction takes place in the past and includes realistic characters, events, and settings. The story may be about real people and actual events. It usually includes dialogue.

🔍 FIND TEXT EVIDENCE

"A Surprise Reunion" is historical fiction. I know that Chief Cameahwait and Sacagawea were real people. The dialogue is fictional since the author could not know what was said during the meeting between Chief Cameahwait and Sacagawea. The historical setting influences the plot because Lewis and Clark depended on the Shoshone to help them explore the land. It was at a meeting Chief Cameahwait had with Captain Clark that Cameahwait is reunited with his sister.

Readers to Writers

When writers use dialogue, they have to imagine what characters sound like when they talk. Try to imagine that you hear your characters' voices when you write dialogue.

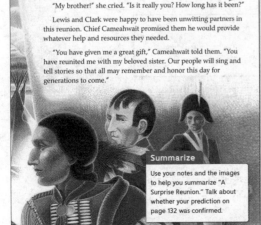

Page 135

Cameahwait could not believe his eyes! He examined the features of her face. He watched as her expression slowly changed. He immediately knew this was the same sweet face of his lost sister.

Sacagawea quickly ran to him. Tears filled her dark eyes. The pain and sadness that Cameahwait had carried over the years **retreated** to a forgotten place.

"My brother!" she cried. "Is it really you? How long has it been?"

Lewis and Clark were happy to have been unwitting partners in this reunion. Chief Cameahwait promised them he would provide whatever help and resources they needed.

"You have given me a great gift," Cameahwait told them. "You have reunited me with my beloved sister. Our people will sing and tell stories so that all may remember and honor this day for generations to come."

Summarize

Use your notes and the images to help you summarize "A Surprise Reunion." Talk about whether your prediction on page 132 was confirmed.

Dialogue

Dialogue is the words the characters speak in the text. Dialogue helps you understand what the characters are thinking and feeling.

Your Turn Review and discuss the characters and events in "A Surprise Reunion." List two examples from the story that show it is historical fiction.

COLLABORATE

_____

_____

_____

_____

Theme

The theme of a text is the overall message or lesson that an author wants to communicate. To identify the theme, think about what the characters do and say and how they change. Pay attention to the characters' thoughts and feelings.

Quick Tip

To identify the theme, you make an inference. Find details that are clues. Then use what you know to identify what the author wants to communicate.

🔍 FIND TEXT EVIDENCE

When I read page 133, I learn that Chief Cameahwait is thinking about his younger sister, who was snatched in a raid. He misses her. I think these details are clues to the story's theme.

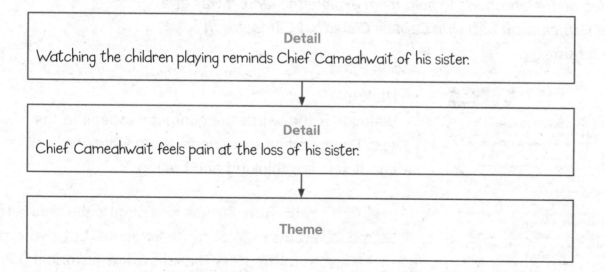

Detail

Watching the children playing reminds Chief Cameahwait of his sister.

⬇

Detail

Chief Cameahwait feels pain at the loss of his sister.

⬇

Theme

Your Turn Reread "A Surprise Reunion." What other details give clues about the theme? List them in the graphic organizer on page 141. Use the details to figure out the theme.

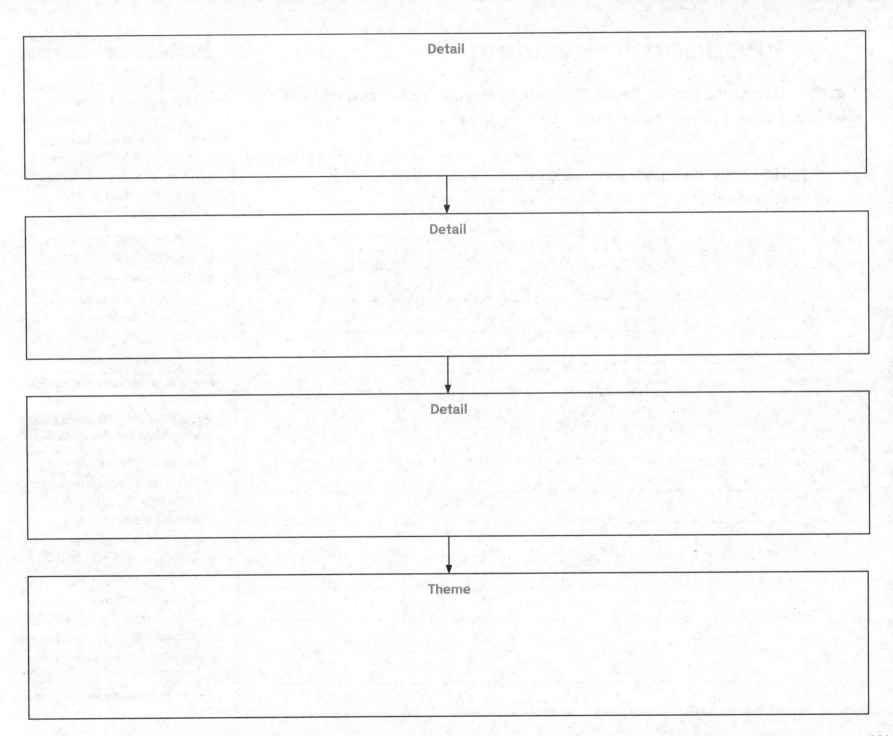

Detail

Detail

Detail

Theme

Respond to Reading

COLLABORATE

Discuss the prompt below. Think about how the author develops the theme. Use your notes and graphic organizer.

How does the author communicate the message that family is important?

_____

_____

_____

_____

_____

_____

_____

_____

_____

_____

_____

_____

_____

Quick Tip

Discuss any questions you have with a partner. This helps you gain information about a text and deepens your understanding. Use these sentence starters to discuss the text and explain your answer.

- _In the beginning, Chief Cameahwait . . ._

- _At a meeting at the Lewis and Clark camp, Chief Cameahwait . . ._

- _In the end, Chief Cameahwait says . . ._

Grammar Connections

Make sure you capitalize the characters' names, including the titles connected with their names. For example: _Chief Cameahwait_ and _Captain Lewis_.

If you are writing a historical text, you must also capitalize historical periods, events, and documents.

Make a Research Plan

A **research plan** helps you manage your time and stay focused on your task. To create a research plan:

- Write down the topic you want to research. Ask a librarian or an adult to assist you with the research.
- Brainstorm places where you can find information related to that topic. Start with a book from your school library or reliable sources on the Internet.
- Make a list of details you want to research.
- Decide if there are any people or organizations you should contact for more information.

Create a question chart. Fill in rows with questions you want answered. Write at least one question for each of these question words: *Who? What? Where? When? Why?* and *How?*

As you look for more information, what visuals could you use to help you with your search?

 Tech Tip

When you start your search on the Internet, put each question in quotes. If other researchers asked the exact same question as you, the quotes will help you find answers more easily. If no information results from your search, then remove the quotes and try again.

COLLABORATE

Write an Encyclopedia Entry Choose a Native American group that lives in your state. Write a research plan to determine where you will learn more about the group and find answers to these questions.

- What are some of the traditions of the group?
- Why did the group settle in that region?
- How long has the group lived there?

Be sure to add a visual to your encyclopedia entry. For example, you might draw or print out a map showing your state and where the group lives.

FatCamera/E+/Getty Images

The Game of Silence

? **What is the author's purpose in telling the reader how difficult and challenging the game of silence is?**

*Literature Anthology:
pages 482–493*

Talk About It Reread **Literature Anthology** page 486. With a partner, talk about why Omakayas struggles to stay quiet during the game.

Cite Text Evidence What details show how challenging the game is for Omakayas? Write text evidence in the chart.

Sensory Details	Why is this effective?

Write The author wants me to understand how difficult and challenging the game is because _____

_____

_____

Make Inferences

Omakayas's cousins have names like Twilight, Little Bee, and Two Strike Girl. What can you infer about the characters from their names?

Quick Tip

When you reread, think about how the author uses sensory details. The sensory details will help you understand how the characters are playing the game.

? How does the author use words and phrases to create a sense of community?

Talk About It Reread **Literature Anthology** page 489. With a partner, talk about how the author describes the lodge and the meal.

Cite Text Evidence What sensory details does the author use to describe the lodge and the meal? Write text evidence in the web below.

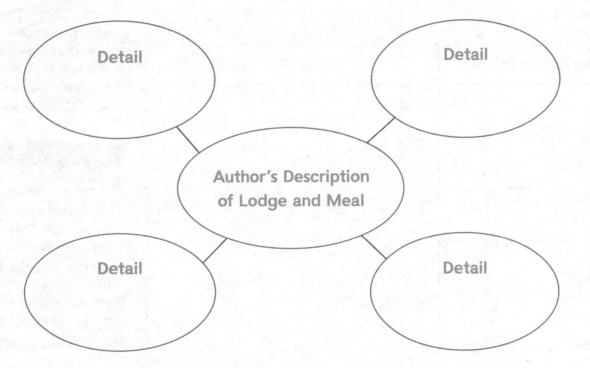

Detail

Detail

Author's Description of Lodge and Meal

Detail

Detail

Write The author uses words and phrases to create a sense of community by _____

_____

_____

Synthesize Information

Think about your home and family. When friends and family visit, how is it similar to Omakayas's family experience? How is it different?

Quick Tip

When you read a story, pay attention to sensory details. Writers often describe the five senses—sights, sounds, touch, tastes, and smells—to help you picture their characters' lives and experiences.

You can use these sentence frames when talking about community.

The author describes the lodge and meal . . .

These descriptions help me visualize . . .

? How does the author show that the Ojibwe value the children in their tribe?

COLLABORATE

Talk About It Reread **Literature Anthology** pages 490–491. With a partner, talk about how the children know that the meeting is important.

Cite Text Evidence How does the author's description of the prizes help you understand what is important to the Ojibwe tribe? Write text evidence below.

Description of the Prizes	What This Shows

Write The author shows that the Ojibwe valued the children in their tribe by _____

_____

_____

Evaluate Information

A historical setting describes a time in the past. A cultural setting describes how a group of people live. The way characters act in a setting develops the plot of the story. What is the setting of "Game of Silence?" How does the historical and cultural setting influence the plot?

Quick Tip

When you reread, visualize the scene the author describes. Picture in your mind how the children act when they get their prizes. This will help you understand the role of the prizes in the tribe.

Respond to Reading

COLLABORATE

Discuss the prompt below. Apply your own knowledge of family and traditions to inform your answer. Use your notes and graphic organizer.

How do you know that family is important to the story's message?

_____

_____

_____

_____

_____

_____

_____

_____

_____

_____

_____

_____

_____

Quick Tip

Use these sentence starters to organize your text evidence.

The author uses words and phrases to help me visualize . . .

The author's descriptions support the story's message because . . .

The sensory details help me understand the theme because . . .

Self-Selected Reading

When you read independently, you read on your own. Choose a text. Read the first few pages to see if it interests you. If not, pick another text and read independently for a sustained period of time. Fill in your writer's notebook with the title, author, genre, and your purpose for reading.

Native Americans: Yesterday and Today

Literature Anthology: pages 496–499

Native Americans of Long Ago

[1]   Yet those ways of life changed once Europeans arrived. Scholars believe thousands, perhaps millions, of Native Americans died from diseases brought by white settlers in the 1700s. As the United States expanded, wars between the settlers and tribes erupted. Of the Native Americans who survived, many retreated from their lands. The rest were forced westward by white settlers and soldiers. The Indian Removal Act of 1830 relocated tribes west of the Mississippi River. This opened up 25 million acres to settlement. Native American groups in all regions had to cope with loss. While adapting to new environments, tribes struggled to maintain traditions.

Circle the strong words the author uses to describe what happened between white settlers and soldiers and the Native Americans. Write three of those words here.

1 _____

2 _____

3 _____

COLLABORATE

Talk with a partner about how life changed for Native Americans after Europeans arrived. How does the author's description help you understand the changes that happened?

_____

_____

_____

Native Americans Today

1   These days, Native people lead different lives from those of their ancestors. Some groups living on reservations face poverty; others have thrived economically. The wild rice that we buy today comes largely from the Ojibwe reservation. The Alabama-Couchattas host over 200,000 people a year at their campgrounds. The Cherokee of Oklahoma have built hotels, hospitals, and entertainment centers. Tourism is an important source of income for the Seminole.

2   Despite what they have endured, Native Americans today maintain ways to honor their culture and history. Dances and gatherings called powwows allow them to celebrate ancient traditions. Sharing stories with each new generation also helps keep the Native American past alive in the present.

Reread paragraph 1. **Underline** the sentence that tells you life for Native Americans today is not like life for Native people in the past. **Circle** the names of Native groups that have thrived economically.

COLLABORATE

Reread paragraph 2. Talk about how Native Americans today honor their cultural traditions. **Make a mark** in the margin beside each clue. Write those two ways here.

1 _____

2 _____

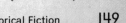

How does the author organize the text to show how life changed for Native Americans?

 Talk About It Reread the two excerpts on pages 148 and 149. With a partner, talk about what you learn about Native Americans under each heading.

Cite Text Evidence Reread the headings for each excerpt. Why are these headings appropriate? Write text evidence in the chart.

Make Inferences

As you reread, compare how the lives of Native Americans have changed from long ago. Why do you think it is important for Native Americans to keep their past alive?

"Native Americans of Long Ago"	"Native Americans Today"

Write The author organizes the text to show how life changed for Native Americans by _____

_____

_____

_____

Maps

Maps are a representation of an area of land or sea. There are many different kinds of maps. Some maps may show the physical characteristics of a land area, the climate of a region, or the products of a location.

Many maps include a title, labels, map key, compass rose, and map scale. A map key shows what the symbols and colors on the map represent. A compass rose shows direction. A map scale is used to find the distance between places.

Historical fiction writers often use maps that show real locations.

 Evaluate Information

Reread where each Native American group originally settled. Then look at the map and evaluate the challenges each group faced in its new environment. Compare and contrast the difference in land and climate of the areas.

FIND TEXT EVIDENCE

On page 497 of "Native Americans: Yesterday and Today," the author includes a map to show where some Native American tribes were relocated to in the mid-1800s. As you read the text, the map shows the areas described in the selection.

Relocation of Native American Tribes

Mississippi River →

Key:
- Ojibwe
- Seminole
- Cherokee
- Alabama-Coushatta

> The Indian Removal Act of 1830 relocated tribes west of the Mississippi River.

 Your Turn Reread pages 497 and 498.

- Look at the map. Which Native American group relocated the farthest north?_____

- Which Native American group relocated the farthest south? _____

_____

Text Connections

? **How does the photographer express a similar point of view about traditions as the authors of "The Game of Silence," "Native Americans: Yesterday and Today," and the Blast "Living Your Past"?**

Talk About It Look at the photograph and read the caption. With a partner, discuss how the photographer shows that traditions are important.

Cite Text Evidence **Circle** clues in the photograph that show both a tradition and a family. **Underline** a phrase in the caption that tells more about how the photograph shows tradition. Think about the selections you read this week. How did the authors use words and phrases to tell their points of view?

Write The photographer's point of view is like those of the selections and the Blast because _____

_____

_____

_____

_____

_____

Coral Coolahan/Getty Images

A Navajo woman teaches her granddaughter the skill of hand-spinning wool.

Quick Tip

Present Your Work

COLLABORATE

When you have completed your research plan, use it to write an encyclopedia entry. In the encyclopedia entry, tell about the Native American group you chose and its relationship to your state.

Discuss how you will present your encyclopedia entry and map or image to the class. With your teacher and classmates, discuss how you can combine your work to make a class reference guide. Use the Presenting Checklist as you practice your presentation. Discuss the sentence starters below and write your answers.

VIKINGS

Introduction
The Vikings were seafaring warriors and explorers from Scandinavia...

Culture
Between the 8th and 11th centuries, Vikings traded with and plundered many European nations...

Viking Ships
Expert sailors, the Vikings reached foreign lands by large wooden boats called longships and knorrs...

An interesting fact I learned about the Native American group is _____

_____

_____

I would like to know more about _____

_____

_____

_____

Quick Tip

If you used a map, make sure it is clearly labeled and easy to read. If you used a photograph or an illustration, be sure to include a caption with additional information about the subject.

✓ Presenting Checklist

☐ Rehearse your presentation in front of a friend. Ask for feedback.

☐ Speak clearly, at an understandable pace and volume. Stop to ask if listeners understand the entry as you present it.

☐ Make eye contact with people in the audience.

☐ Point to key parts of your map or image as you describe it.

☐ Listen carefully to questions from the audience.

David Vernon/Getty Images

Essential Question

What shapes a person's identity?

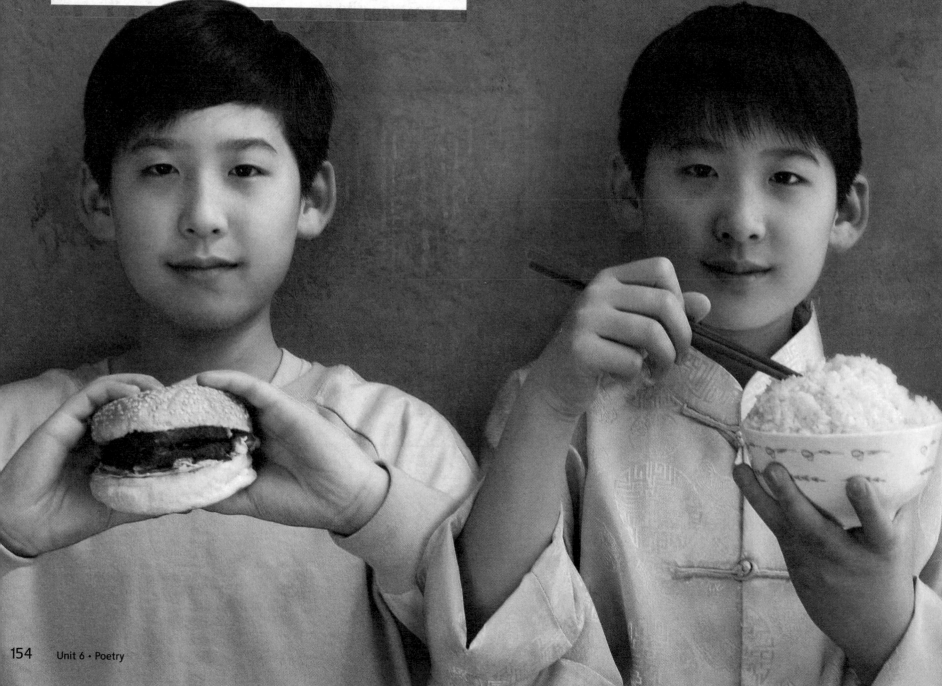

COLLABORATE

The people in your life help shape who you are, yet you are unique. Think about the people around you, such as your family and friends. How are you like them? How are you different from them?

Talk with a partner about things that shape a person's identity. What makes you who you are? Write words from your discussion in the chart.

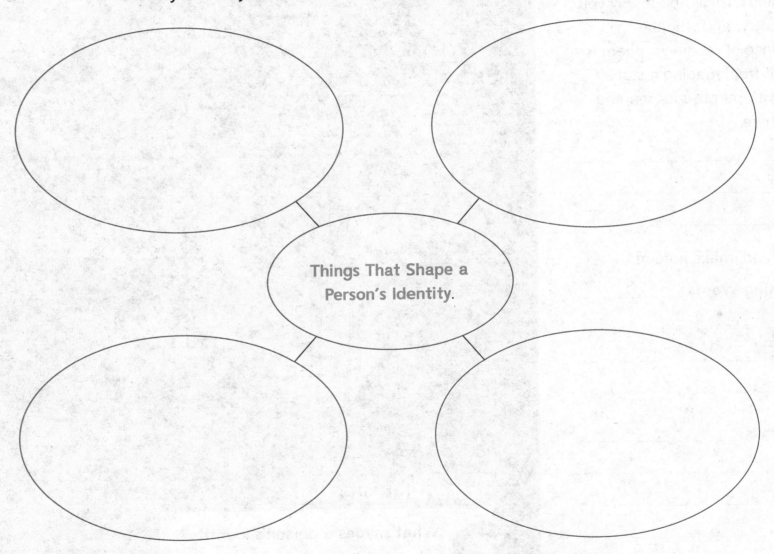

Things That Shape a Person's Identity.

BLAST BACK!
studysync

Go online to **my.mheducation.com** and read the "Becoming Bessie" Blast. Think about how you are finding your place in the world. Then blast back your response.

Simon Marcus Taplin/Corbis/Getty Images

SHARED READ

TAKE NOTES

Read the titles and look at the illustrations. Think about why you read poetry, and why the experience of reading a poem is different from reading a story. Write your purpose for reading poetry here.

_____

_____

_____

As you read, make note of:

Interesting Words_____

_____

_____

_____

Key Details_____

_____

_____

_____

Essential Question

? **What shapes a person's identity?**

Read to discover how poets talk about important experiences.

156   Unit 6 • Poetry

CLIMBING BLUE HILL

When the yellow leaves begin to
glimmer among the green ones,
we hike up Blue Hill
through an early morning mist.

"It's not much farther, boys!"
My grandfather bellows happily,
his words an echo of all the other times
he's had to urge us up a steep trail.

I hear the comforting squeak of his boots
as the ground's chill breath whispers
against our ankles and the overgrown
branches tug curiously at my hair.

Abruptly, the trail spits us out,
onto gray rock, into blue sky and sunlight.
My brother shouts, shoves me aside,
races to the low bushes huddled against the wind.

His fingers tug at the tiny leaves.
"Look! Blueberries!" He yells.
And we gobble the blue sweetness up,
my brother, my grandfather, and me.

— Andrew Feher

(tr) Tim Grollimund; (bkgd) Stephen Frink/Corbis

FIND TEXT EVIDENCE

Read

Stanzas 1–5
Free Verse

What makes this poem a free verse poem?

_____

_____

_____

_____

Stanza 4
Personification

Draw a box around an example of how the trail acts like a person.
Underline an example of how the bushes act like humans.

Reread

Author's Craft

What images does the poet use to help you understand how he feels about hiking with his grandfather?

FIND TEXT EVIDENCE

Read

Stanzas 1–3

Imagery

Circle the words that help you picture what ivy looks like.

Personification

Stanzas 4–5

Draw a box around the words that tell how ivy acts like a person.

Theme

Why was Ivy given the name of a plant? Write your answer.

_____

_____

_____

_____

Reread

Author's Craft

How does the poet's word choice help you visualize the ivy?

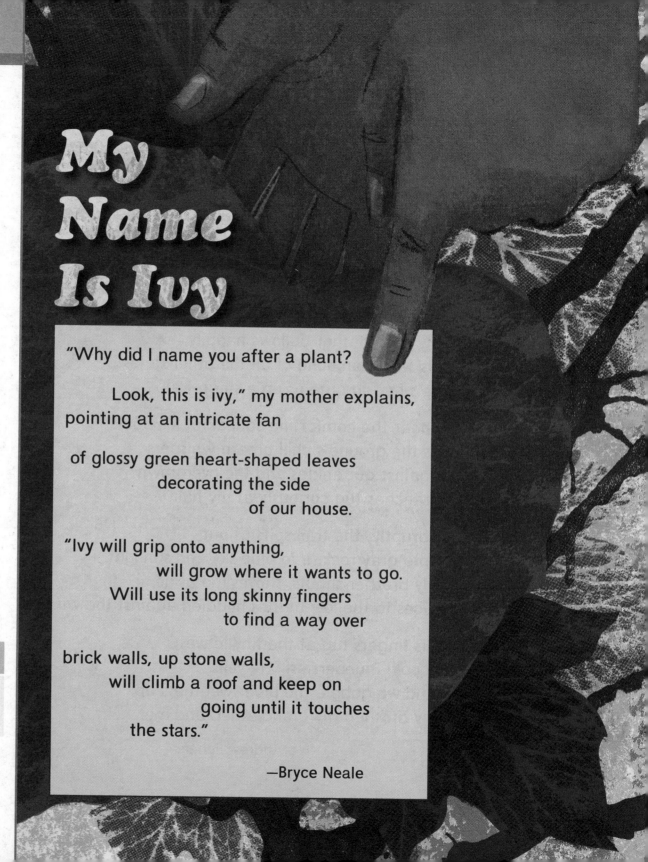

My Name Is Ivy

"Why did I name you after a plant?

　　Look, this is ivy," my mother explains,
pointing at an intricate fan

of glossy green heart-shaped leaves
　　　　decorating the side
　　　　　　　of our house.

"Ivy will grip onto anything,
　　　　will grow where it wants to go.
　　Will use its long skinny fingers
　　　　　　to find a way over

brick walls, up stone walls,
　　will climb a roof and keep on
　　　　　going until it touches
　　the stars."

—Bryce Neale

Collage

Grandma gave me her eyes.
"Eyes of a panther," Grandpa whispers.

Grandpa gave me his nose.
"A bumpy, rocky road of a nose," Grandma scoffs.

Dad gave me his long skinny toes.
"My roots reach back to the lemurs," he jokes.

Mama gave me her lopsided smile.
"Don't ever lose it," she warns.

And I gave them my heart.
"It's big enough to hold you all," I say.

— Maria Diaz

Make Connections

Compare how the poets were influenced by different people in their lives. Who has influenced you? Discuss your influences with a partner.

FIND TEXT EVIDENCE

Read

Stanzas 1–3

Metaphor

Underline the words that use a comparison to show what Grandma's eyes are like.
Draw a box around the words that use a comparison to show what Grandpa's nose is like.

Stanzas 4–5

Theme

Circle the words that show how the speaker feels about her family. What does this tell you about the speaker? Write the answer.

_____

_____

Reread

Author's Craft

How does the poet use repetition in the poem? How does it help you understand how the people in the speaker's family have shaped her?

Vocabulary

Use the example sentences to talk with a partner about each word. Then answer the questions.

gobble

The hungry dogs **gobble** up their dinner quickly.

What other animals might gobble up a meal?

_____

_____

individuality

Sarita showed her **individuality** by putting glitter on her plain slippers.

How do you show your individuality?

_____

_____

mist

The spray from the sprinklers created a wet **mist**.

What things can produce a mist?

_____

_____

roots

My family has **roots** in California, but most of our family lives in Florida.

What have you learned about your roots?

_____

_____

Poetry Terms

metaphor

A **metaphor** compares two unlike things without using the words _like_ or _as_.

Use a metaphor to describe a cloud.

_____

_____

personification

Personification is when human characteristics are given to anything that is not human.

What would be an example of personification?

_____

_____

imagery

Imagery is the use of words to create a picture in the reader's mind.

How would using sensory details help to create imagery in a poem?

_____

_____

free verse

Free verse poems do not have a consistent metrical pattern or rhyme scheme.

Why might a poet choose to write in free verse?

_____

_____

> **Build Your Word List** Reread the second stanza on page 158. Use a print or online dictionary to help you find synonyms for the word *intricate.* In your writer's notebook, make a word web for the synonyms.

Figurative Language

A **metaphor** is a comparison of two unlike things without the use of the words *like* or *as*.

🔍 **FIND TEXT EVIDENCE**

To find a metaphor, I need to look for two unlike things that are being compared. In the poem "Collage" on page 159, the grandmother compares the grandfather's nose to a road.

Grandpa gave me his nose.
"A bumpy, rocky road of a nose,"
Grandma scoffs.

Your Turn Reread "My Name Is Ivy" on page 158. What is the main metaphor in the poem?

_____

_____

_____

Imagery and Personification

Imagery is the use of specific language to create a picture in a reader's mind. **Personification** is giving human qualities to something non-human, such as an animal or an object.

FIND TEXT EVIDENCE

I can find examples of imagery and personification when I reread the poem "Climbing Blue Hill" on page 157.

on page 157

> When the yellow leaves begin to
> glimmer among the green ones,
> we hike up Blue Hill
> through an early morning mist. . . .
>
> I hear the comforting squeak of his boots
> as the ground's chill breath whispers
> against our ankles and the overgrown
> branches tug curiously at my hair.

Imagery

The lines *When the yellow leaves begin to/ glimmer among the green ones* are an example of imagery.

Personification

The lines *as the ground's chill breath whispers/ against our ankles* are an example of personification.

Quick Tip

To help you understand the meaning of the poem, read aloud the stanzas one at a time to a partner. Ask your partner to retell what happens in each stanza. Then exchange roles with your partner.

Your Turn Work with a partner to find an example of imagery and personification in the poem "My Name Is Ivy."

_____

_____

_____

Free Verse

A **free verse** poem does not follow the usual rules of poetry. It does not have a rhyme scheme or metrical pattern. A free verse poem may have irregular lines.

FIND TEXT EVIDENCE

I can tell that "My Name Is Ivy" is a free verse poem because it does not have a rhyme scheme or metrical pattern.

Page 158

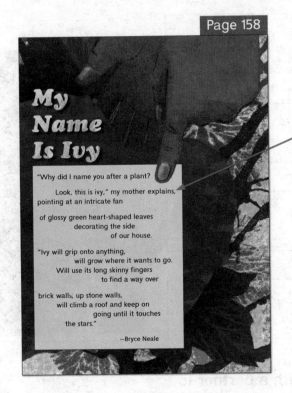

My Name Is Ivy

"Why did I name you after a plant?
    Look, this is ivy," my mother explains,
pointing at an intricate fan

of glossy green heart-shaped leaves
        decorating the side
                of our house.

"Ivy will grip onto anything,
        will grow where it wants to go.
    Will use its long skinny fingers
            to find a way over

brick walls, up stone walls,
        will climb a roof and keep on
                going until it touches
    the stars."

—Bryce Neale

Readers to Writers

When poets write a free verse poem, they think about how it looks on the page as much as how it sounds when read aloud. When you write a free verse poem, think about how you want it to look and rewrite it in that form.

I wonder why the lines are all spread out. The lines in this poem are not the same length. The poet chose to give the lines a zigzag pattern. Maybe the poet is showing how the words climb the page the way ivy climbs a wall.

Your Turn With a partner, reread the poem "Collage" on page 159. Explain what makes it a free verse poem.

COLLABORATE

_____

_____

_____

Theme

The theme is the main message or lesson in a poem. Identifying the key details in a poem can help you determine the theme.

🔍 **FIND TEXT EVIDENCE**

All of the poems in this lesson are about identity, but each poem has a different theme. I'll reread "Collage" on page 159 and look for key details to determine the theme of the poem.

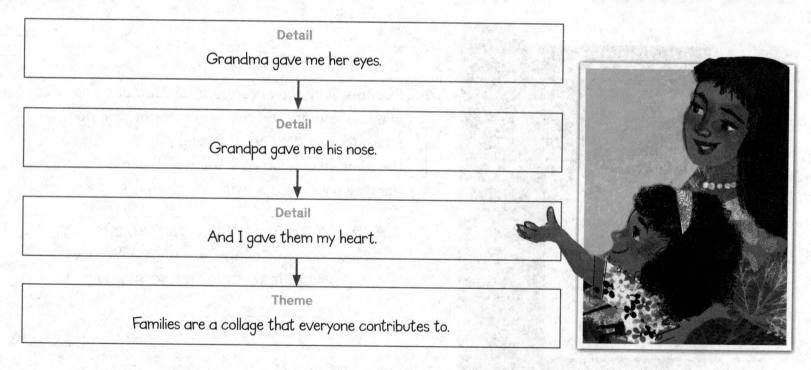

Detail
Grandma gave me her eyes.

↓

Detail
Grandpa gave me his nose.

↓

Detail
And I gave them my heart.

↓

Theme
Families are a collage that everyone contributes to.

COLLABORATE

Your Turn Read "My Name Is Ivy" on page 158. Work with a partner to find the key details and list them in the graphic organizer on page 165. Use the details to determine the theme of the poem.

Quick Tip

The theme is expressed in a sentence or several sentences, not just one word. To identify the theme, look for the details that describe the people in the poem and their actions.

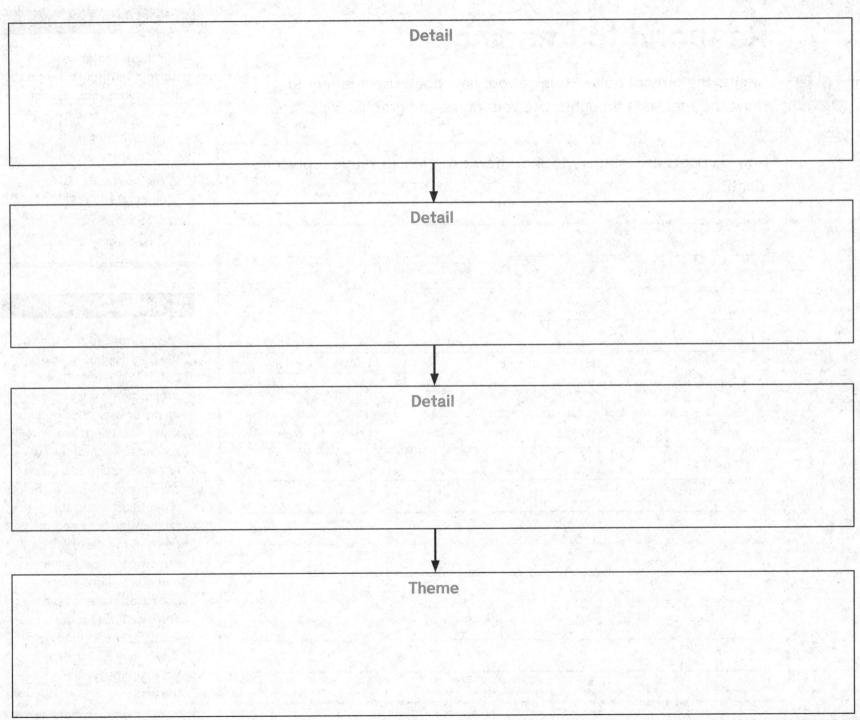

Detail

Detail

Detail

Theme

Respond to Reading

COLLABORATE

Discuss the prompt below. Think about how poets use imagery to show the speaker's thoughts. Use your notes and graphic organizer.

How do poets use imagery to show how experiences shape a person's identity?

_____

_____

_____

_____

_____

_____

_____

_____

_____

_____

_____

Quick Tip

Use these sentence starters to discuss the text and explain your answer.

- *In the poem, the poet writes about the experience of . . .*

- *The poet uses sensory language to create imagery, such as . . .*

- *This imagery shows . . .*

Grammar Connections

As you write your response, use prepositions to add detail. Remember that a preposition is a word like *in, on,* or *after.* Prepositions show how things are related to each other. For example, a pen can be *on* or *under* or *in* a desk. The preposition shows the relationship between the pen and the desk. You can use prepositions as you describe the imagery the poet uses. For example, *The ivy climbs up the wall.* The preposition *up* shows the relationship between the ivy and the wall.

SCIENCE

Conduct an Interview

When you **interview** someone, you ask the person questions about a specific topic. For example, you can interview an adult about his or her job. Or you can interview a friend or family member. When you interview a friend or family member, you don't have to be as formal as when you interview someone you don't know. Here are some tips for conducting an interview:

- In a notebook, make a list of questions you want to ask.
- Bring a recording device to record the interview.
- Take notes while you listen to the speaker.

Who is someone you'd like to interview? What topic or topics would you like to discuss? Write your answer.

_____

_____

COLLABORATE

Create a Podcast With a partner, discuss traits you share with members of your family. Include traits that are inherited, or passed down from family members, such as eye color or hair color. Also include learned traits, such as playing sports or reading well. Then choose a family member to interview about inherited or learned traits in your family.

With your partner, prepare a list of formal questions beforehand. Review your questions to make sure they are clear. Bring a recording device so you can capture the quotes you'll need for your podcast.

> **Tech Tip**
>
> You can use a laptop, tablet, or cell phone as a recording device. Before you start recording, check where you want to place your device to get a clear recording. Remember to ask permission of the person being interviewed before you begin recording.

dolgachov/iStock/Getty Images

Birdfoot's Grampa

 How does the poet's use of imagery make readers care about what happens to the toads?

Literature Anthology: pages 500–505

 Talk About It Reread stanza 3 on page 501 of the **Literature Anthology**. Talk with a partner about what you visualize in this last stanza.

Cite Text Evidence Identify words and phrases used by the poet to paint a picture of Grampa saving the toads. What do these words and phrases say about Grampa's hands and the toads? Write text evidence.

 Make Inferences

The speaker says, "You can't save them all" to the grandfather. What can you infer about how the speaker feels about saving toads at the end of the poem?

Sensory Language	Why This Is Effective

Quick Tip

When I reread, I can think about how the poet describes the characters and events. I look for specific words the poet uses to create an image.

Write The poet's use of imagery makes readers care about what happens to the toads by _____

_____

_____

My Chinatown

 How does the poet's description of the sewing machine help you understand the relationship between the speaker and the mother?

 Talk About It With a partner, reread "My Chinatown" on page 502. Turn to your partner and talk about why the poet compares the mother's work on the sewing machine to a lullaby.

Cite Text Evidence Describe how the poet uses the sewing machine to tell how the speaker feels about her mother's work. Write text evidence in the web to tell if the sewing machine is upsetting or comforting.

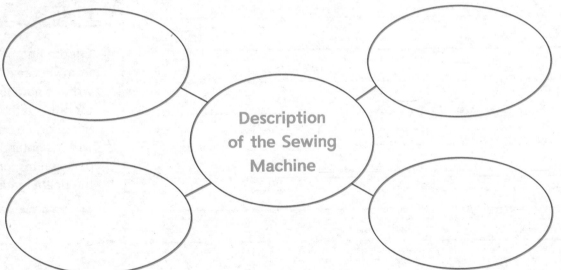

Description of the Sewing Machine

Write The poet's description of the sewing machine helps me understand

_____

_____

_____

Quick Tip

To describe something, an author can use literal or figurative language. Literal language is the dictionary meaning of a word. In figurative language, words are used in a different way from their usual meanings. Figurative language can be used to help readers visualize something. When you reread, look for sensory words the poet uses to describe the sewing machine. Then think about what these words tell you about the speaker and the mother.

 Synthesize Information

Think about the poems "Birdfoot's Grandpa" and "My Chinatown." What do the poems have in common? How do the speakers feel about their parent or grandparent? Describe the similarities.

Respond to Reading

Discuss the prompt below. Apply your own knowledge of family and traditions to inform your answer. Use your notes and graphic organizer.

How do the poets use imagery to communicate how the things people do shape who they are?

_____

_____

_____

_____

_____

_____

_____

_____

_____

_____

_____

Quick Tip

Use these sentence starters to organize your text evidence.

• *The poets use words and phrases to . . .*

• *The poet creates imagery so that . . .*

• *The imagery helps me understand that . . .*

Self-Selected Reading

Choose another poem from your text. In your writer's notebook, write the title, author, and genre of the poem. In your writer's notebook, write a personal response on how the poem made you feel.

Growing Up

? In the poem "Growing Up," on page 504 of the Literature Anthology, how does the poet use words and phrases to help you understand the poem's message?

Literature Anthology: pages 504–505

Talk About It With a partner, identify the speaker in the poem. Discuss how the poet lets the reader know when the mother is speaking.

Cite Text Evidence What words and phrases help you know what the speaker in the poem is like? Write text evidence in the chart.

Quick Tip

When I reread, I can ask myself, *What lesson is the poet trying to teach me about life? What lesson does M'ija learn?*

Text Evidence	What I Visualize

Write I understand the message because the poet uses words and phrases to _____

_____

_____

My People

? **How does Langston Hughes use comparisons to communicate a message?**

Talk About It Reread "My People" on page 505. With a partner, talk about what you visualize when you read the poet's comparisons.

Cite Text Evidence What strong comparisons does the poet make? What is the poet saying about all of these things? Write text evidence in the chart.

Quick Tip

When you reread, pay attention to the way the poet uses figurative language. Notice how the poet describes each object being compared. For example, you can picture the twinkling of stars as well as the twinkling in people's eyes. Comparing the beauty of each thing with people's eyes, faces, and souls helps you understand the poet's message.

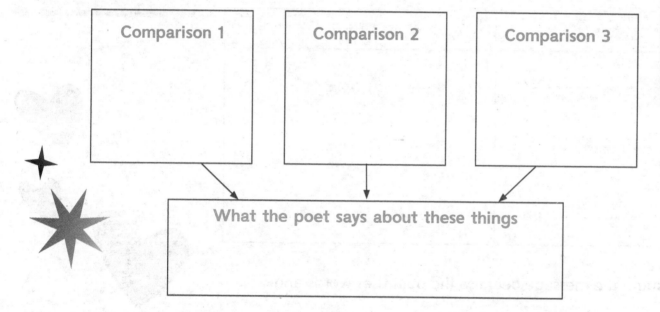

Comparison 1	Comparison 2	Comparison 3

What the poet says about these things

Write The poet uses comparisons to communicate a message about _____

_____

_____

_____

Voice

Read "Growing Up" on page 504 of the **Literature Anthology** aloud and listen for the author's **voice**. Voice shows how a writer feels about a topic. Voice is what gives a character a specific personality. The writer chooses language that shows the characters' thoughts and feelings.

 FIND TEXT EVIDENCE

In the poem, a mother and daughter speak. The poet's use of language gives each speaker a distinct voice. The daughter's voice is simple and direct: *I want to be a doctor.* The mother's voice is caring: *you will patch scraped knees/ and wipe away children's tears.*

> When I grow up,
> I want to be a doctor.
>
> *M'ija, you will patch scraped knees*
> *and wipe away children's tears.*

Your Turn Reread the last three stanzas of the poem "Growing Up."

- How does the mother's voice change at the end of the poem? _____

_____

_____

- How does the daughter's voice change at the end of the poem? _____

_____

_____

When you write poems, think about what feelings you want to express in the poem. What voice or personality do you want your poem to have? Use sensory language to create images in the reader's mind. Remember, sensory words and phrases are ones that appeal to your five senses (sight, sound, taste, touch, smell).

Text Connections

? How does Henry Wadsworth Longfellow help you visualize what influenced Hiawatha's life? How is Wadsworth's use of imagery similar to imagery used by the other poets you read this week? In what ways are the themes of the "Becoming Bessie" Blast and this week's poems similar?

Talk About It Read "Hiawatha's Childhood." Talk with a partner about what Hiawatha did.

Cite Text Evidence **Underline** words and phrases that show Hiawatha's actions. **Circle** how you know how Hiawatha feels about the animals.

Write Henry Wadsworth Longfellow's use of imagery is like _____

_____

_____

_____

_____

Design Pics/Jason Witherspoon

Quick Tip

Look for words and phrases that describe what was important to Hiawatha. Then you can compare "Hiawatha's Childhood" to the other poems you read this week. You can ask, *What does Hiawatha do? What does this show about his identity? How do characters in other poems show their identity?*

Hiawatha's Childhood

Of all beasts he learned the language,
Learned their names and all their secrets,
How the beavers built their lodges,
Where the squirrels hid their acorns,
How the reindeer ran so swiftly,
Why the rabbit was so timid,
Talked with them whene'er he met them,
Called them "Hiawatha's Brothers."

— Henry Wadsworth Longfellow

Accuracy and Phrasing

When you read free verse poems, **accuracy** (or being precise) is important. Look up the pronunciation of any unfamiliar words and practice them until you can read the poem with accuracy. Then read carefully to make sure you don't leave out any words.

Because free verse doesn't follow the same rules as other forms of poetry, **phrasing** (grouping words to make a poem sound natural and interesting) is also a very important part of reading. You don't have to pause at the end of every line of free verse. Some lines are meant to flow together. Pause at the commas or periods, not the end of every line.

Page 157

"It's not much farther, boys!"
My grandfather bellows happily,
his words an echo of all the other times
he's had to urge us up a steep trail.

Pause longest at the exclamation point and period.

Pause briefly at the comma.

Quick Tip

Before reading a poem aloud, review the pronunciations of unfamiliar words. Look up the word's pronunciation in a dictionary or listen to its pronunciation and syllabication using an online dictionary. Pronounce the word and read aloud each syllable clearly. Then take your time as you read a poem aloud. Remember to pause at punctuation marks.

Your Turn Turn back to page 157. Practice reading challenging words with a partner. Next, circle the punctuation marks to remind you to pause briefly at each one. Then take turns reading "Climbing Blue Hill" aloud with your partner.

Afterward, think about how you did. Complete these sentences.

I remembered to _____

Next time, I will _____

Expert Model

Literature Anthology pages 500–501

Free verse is a form of poetry that ignores the rules of rhythm, meter, and rhyme. The poet chooses words that create images a reader will be able to picture. A free verse poem may contain other literary elements.

- It may have figurative language, such as metaphors and similes.

- There may be alliteration, repetition of the same sounds at the beginning of words.

- It may use precise or sensory words.

Analyze an Expert Model Studying free verse poems will help you learn how to write a free verse poem. **Reread** "Birdfoot's Grampa" on page 501 of the **Literature Anthology**. Write your answers below.

How can you tell that "Birdfoot's Grampa" is a free verse poem?

_____

_____

How does the poet use precise and sensory words to help the

reader picture an image in the poem? _____

_____

_____

Word Wise

On page 501, the author uses words to paint pictures, such as *a mist about his white hair* and *knee deep in the summer roadside grass.* This helps bring readers into the moment of the poem and gives them a greater connection to the experience.

Bonee/Shutterstock.com

Plan: Choose Your Topic

Freewrite Think about a person who is important to you. On the lines below, write quickly about how that person makes you feel and why that person is important to you.

_____

_____

_____

_____

Writing Prompt Write a free verse poem about the person who is important to you.

I chose _____ because _____.

Purpose and Audience An author's purpose is his or her main reason for writing. Look at the three purposes for writing below. Underline your purpose for writing a free verse poem.

to inform, or teach   to persuade, or convince   to entertain

Think about the audience for your poem. Who will read or hear it?

My audience will be _____.

I will use _____ language when I write my poem.

 Plan In your writer's notebook, make an Idea Web to plot out details about the person you are writing about in your poem. Fill in the circles with characteristics of the person.

Quick Tip

To describe the person you chose, think about what makes the person special to you. Ask yourself these questions:

What does the person look and sound like?

What does the person do that shows who he or she is?

What activities have you done together?

What is a great memory you have of the person?

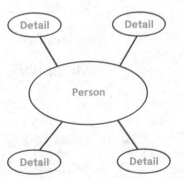

Plan: Metaphor and Simile

Figurative Language Poets use figurative language to create pictures for their readers by comparing things in interesting ways. A **simile** is a figure of speech that compares two things using the words *like* or *as*. For example: *The new grass is like a carpet that tickles my toes*. By using a simile to compare the grass to a carpet that tickles your toes, the poet creates a sensory and more interesting picture for the reader.

Some comparisons don't use *like* or *as*. They are called **metaphors**. For example: *His heart was a hard stone*. Comparing a person's heart to a stone creates a picture of a mean and thoughtless person.

Think about the person that will be the subject of your poem.

Write two similes and two metaphors about that person. You can compare the person's physical features, actions, and sounds with different things.

Simile _____

Simile _____

Metaphor _____

Metaphor _____

_____

Take Notes Once you know what figurative language you would like to use, add more details in your chart. You don't have to write the entire comparison, just use a few key words to remind you when you are ready to write.

michaeljung/iStock/Getty Images

Draft

Alliteration Alliteration is a tool poets use to make language more interesting. In alliteration, the poet uses the same beginning consonant sound in a line or verse. Say the following sentences aloud to see how fun alliteration can be.

> Like a little puppy,
> my little sister Lily
> leaps into the living room.
> I look at the loving smile on her face.

Grammar Connections

Remember to use prepositions to add details to your poem. For example, you can use prepositions such as *in, on,* and *around* to tell where the person is when he or she does certain things. *Flora fell on the frozen ice. Sailors hum songs when they sail across the sea.*

Now use the above sentences as a model to write 2 to 3 lines for your free verse poem about the person who is important to you. Try to include alliteration in each line.

_____

_____

_____

_____

Write a Draft Use your Idea Web and notes to help you write a draft of your free verse poem in your writer's notebook. Remember to paint a picture of your important person for your readers. Imagine how you can show readers exactly what it is like to spend time with the person. Remember to include similes, metaphors, and alliteration in your poem.

Revise

Precise Words Poets use precise words so readers will be able to picture the subject clearly. Read the sentences below. Then revise one or more words in each of the sentences to make them more precise. A thesaurus can help you find the precise word you need.

Quick Tip

When you go back to revise your draft, you may need to add more precise or sensory words. Try to include alliteration and figurative language.

What a day at the beach.

A girl was playing in the sand.

A boy was flying a kite,

and the wind blew it.

I put my feet in the water.

It was a good day.

_____

_____

_____

_____

_____

Revision Revise your draft, and check that you have used precise words and phrases to describe your important person. Also, be sure you included alliteration, metaphors, and similes to make the language in your poem descriptive and interesting.

Image Source/Getty Images

Peer Conferences

COLLABORATE

Review a Draft Listen carefully as a partner reads his or her work aloud. Take notes about what you liked and what was difficult to follow. Begin by telling what you liked about the draft. Ask questions that will help the writer think more about the writing. Make suggestions that you think will make the writing stronger. Use these sentence starters:

I enjoy the way you describe how things sounded and looked because . . .

Another detail about the person you might add is . . .

Can you add some words that show me more about . . . ?

I don't understand this metaphor. Can you explain why . . . ?

Partner Feedback After your partner gives you feedback on your draft, write one of the suggestions that you will use in your revision. Refer to the rubric on page 183 as you give feedback.

Based on my partner's feedback, I will _____

_____

_____

After you finish giving each other feedback, reflect on the peer conference. What was helpful? What might you do differently next time?

Revision As you revise your draft, use the Revising Checklist to help you figure out what text you may need to move, elaborate on, or delete. Remember to use the rubric on page 183 to help with your revision.

Revising Checklist

☐ Does my poem give the reader a good picture of the person I am describing?

☐ Have I included alliteration?

☐ Did I use metaphors and similes to help readers picture the person?

☐ Could my language be more precise?

Edit and Proofread

When you **edit** and **proofread** your writing, you look for and correct mistakes in spelling, punctuation, capitalization, and grammar. Reading through a revised draft multiple times can help you make sure you are catching any errors. Use a thesaurus and the checklist below to edit your sentences.

✔ Editing Checklist

☐ Is there a space between the stanzas?

☐ Is there noun and verb agreement?

☐ Are prepositions used correctly?

☐ Are punctuation marks used correctly?

☐ Are all words spelled correctly?

List two mistakes you found as you proofread your essay.

1 _____

_____

_____

2 _____

_____

_____

Tech Tip

Thesauruses are useful tools for finding precise words. But you should always double check to make sure the words make sense in your poem. Many online thesauruses have a link to an online dictionary. So you can click on a word to find its definition.

Grammar Connections

Possessive nouns often have an apostrophe (') and an *s*. For example, if you want to say that the book belongs to the girl, you would write: *the girl's book*. If a plural noun ends in *s*, the apostrophe goes after the *s*. For example, you would write: *the two girls' book*. The possessive form of *it* does not have an apostrophe. For example, if you want to say that the tail belongs to it, you would write: *its tail*. The word *it's* means "it is."

Publish, Present, and Evaluate

Publishing As you write your final draft, be sure to write legibly in cursive. Check that you are holding your pencil or pen correctly between your forefinger and thumb. This will help you **publish** a neat final copy.

Presentation When you are ready to **present** your work, rehearse reading your poem aloud for a friend. Use the Presenting Checklist to help you.

Evaluate After you publish your writing, use the rubric below to **evaluate** your writing.

What did you do successfully? _____

What needs more work? _____

✔ **Presenting Checklist**

☐ Stand or sit up straight.

☐ Speak clearly and with expression.

☐ Make sure your reading rate matches the feelings you are describing.

☐ Gesture as you read figurative language to help listeners visualize.

4	3	2	1
• effectively uses figurative language to create a clear image of the subject of the poem	• uses some figurative language to create an image of the subject of the poem	• uses little figurative language that doesn't create an image of the subject of the poem	• uses no figurative language
• has many rich details about the subject	• has some details about the subject	• has few details about the subject	• has few details about the subject
• includes several uses of alliteration	• includes some uses of alliteration	• includes little use of alliteration	• includes no alliteration
• has few or no errors in spelling or punctuation	• has some errors in spelling and punctuation	• has frequent errors that might confuse the reader	• has many errors that make it difficult to follow

Spiral Review

You have learned new skills and strategies in Unit 6 that will help you read more critically. Now it is time to practice what you have learned.

- **Dialogue**
- **Imagery**
- **Greek Prefixes**
- **Make Inferences**
- **Main Idea and Key Details**
- **Sidebars**
- **Theme**

Connect to Content

- **Write Historical Fiction**
- **Read Digitally**

Read the selection and choose the best answer to each question.

Renewable and Nonrenewable ENERGY

[1]   The grasses across the plains dance to the rhythm of nature. Back and forth they move, as if to a song only for them. As the winds pick up, a steady *whoosh-whoosh-whoosh* can be heard. These beats are the blades of wind turbines. Nature and machine, together, produce an energetic symphony of sound—and power.

[2]   Natural resources have provided power for thousands of years. Some of these resources can be renewed in a short amount of time. Others are nonrenewable, or cannot be replaced quickly.

Oil

[3]   Have you seen a driver fill up a gas tank? Petroleum products such as gas are made from crude oil, a nonrenewable resource. Formed by animals and plants that lived millions of years ago, crude oil is found as liquid in pools under the ground and within rocks. After the oil is drilled, it is sent to a refinery to produce petroleum. People rely on this resource to fuel their vehicles, heat their homes, and make medical supplies and plastics.

Spaces Images/Blend Images

U.S. Energy Consumption by Energy Source, 2015

Total = 97.7 quadrillion British thermal units

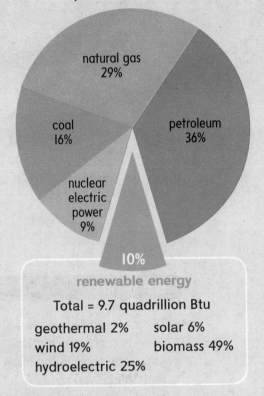

- natural gas 29%
- petroleum 36%
- coal 16%
- nuclear electric power 9%
- 10% renewable energy

Total = 9.7 quadrillion Btu

geothermal 2% solar 6%
wind 19% biomass 49%
hydroelectric 25%

Americans use a variety of energy resources. Notice that the majority of the energy in the United States still comes from nonrenewable resources. If the United States continues to explore renewable resources, how might this pie graph be different in 2035?

Source: U.S. Energy Information Administration, *Monthly Energy Review*, Table 1.3 and 10.1 (April 2016), preliminary data

Natural Gas

4   Natural gas is also found under ground in shale and in the large cracks and spaces between rocks. It is a nonrenewable energy source that was formed millions of years ago. Natural gas is the second most popular energy source in the U.S. Drills dig into the Earth and allow the natural gas to flow to the surface. Then the gases are separated and sent through a pipeline. Some experts estimate that the U.S. has enough natural gas to last 93 more years.

Hydropower

5   Water power, or <u>hydropower</u>, is one of the most popular renewable energy sources in the United States. The volume, or amount, of water draining into streams and rivers affects how much power is produced. The rate that water flows also affects the amount of power produced. A steady flow of water makes more energy than water moving slowly.

Wind Power

6   Wind power is a renewable energy source. The wind pushes the blades of a wind turbine. The blades connect to a tall shaft and then to a generator, which makes electricity. In 2016, around 5 percent of U.S. electric power came from wind. That is enough power for almost 17.5 million homes. Texas, Iowa, Kansas, Oklahoma, and California produce about half of all the U.S. wind electricity.

Energy Resources and Conservation

7   We can conserve, or save, energy so we don't run out. Walk or ride a bike instead of riding in a motor vehicle. Turn off lights when not in use. Every little bit will help!

1 The Greek prefix *hydro-* means "water." This information helps the reader know that the word <u>hydropower</u> in paragraph 5 means —

   A power gained from water

   B wind power needed to make water flow

   C water that flows at a slow rate

   D power that makes water

2 What is the purpose of the sidebar on page 185?

   F to show how much natural gas the United States produces

   G to explain renewable and nonrenewable resources

   H to show the resources that the United States consumes

   J to explain how hydropower is generated in the United States

3 The detail that supports the main idea that people need to conserve nonrenewable resources is —

   A People rely on this resource to fuel their vehicles.

   B Natural gas is the second most popular energy source.

   C In 2016, around 5 percent of U.S. electric power came from wind.

   D The U.S. has enough natural gas to last 93 more years.

4 What inference can be made about the article?

   F Scientists are exploring various types of resources for power.

   G Scientists do not know how many energy sources are available.

   H Scientists have stopped discovering new ways to gain power.

   J Scientists think nonrenewable energy is the most practical.

> **Quick Tip**
>
> Diagrams and other visuals provide more information about the topic in the main text. When you read, review the visuals and information in sidebars to help you better understand the topic.

Read the selection and choose the best answer to each question.

Fighting for the Alamo

1   My father, the deputy sheriff, announced, "Adina De Zavala imprisoned herself at the Alamo! She said, 'I'll stay here forever if needs be.'" Then my father muttered to himself, "Forever, huh? Let's see how long forever is without food and her beloved coffee!"

2   For the past several years, an ex-teacher, Adina De Zavala, had worked relentlessly to preserve historic landmarks in Texas, including the Alamo—"the scene of a siege and battle during the Texas Revolution in 1836." Now, she had locked herself in the old building in order to prevent it from being sold or demolished.

3   Being the son of a San Antonio deputy sheriff, and a marshal, meant that I had to uphold the law. But was withholding food from someone who stands up for what she believes *lawful*?

4   "*Psst!* Ms. De Zavala?" I whispered. "Are you there?"

5   Around midnight, I sneaked down to the Alamo like a thief on the hunt. The Alamo was not in the best condition—there was a dank, musty odor in the air. She wanted to preserve *this*?

6   I glanced up toward the second floor and spotted Ms. De Zavala.

7   "Yes? Who's there?"

8   "Good evening, Ma'am. It's me, Tim Garrity. I heard you're refusing to come out, and I was just wondering, how are you faring?"

9   "Good evening, Mr. Garrity. I would be telling a falsehood if I said my accommodations were comfortable. Criminals fare better in the town jail with beds and food. But at least I have electricity again. Those rats last night scared me more than fighting in the Texas Revolution with only a frying pan! If this is what it takes to protect this place, then I'll stay forever if needs be. What can I do for you at this hour?"

10   "I managed a few sandwiches from our pantry. Hungry?"

11   "Famished! How can we get the sandwiches all the way up here, though?"

12   "I thought of that, too," I said, opening my satchel and taking out the sturdy cord left over from our yard swing. I tossed it up to Ms. De Zavala. She tied it around a bannister and threw down the end. Then I secured the sandwiches, and she pulled them up with the cord.

13   As she started eating, I asked, "Ma'am, why do you care about all of these old buildings in Texas anyway? The Alamo is falling down!"

14   "I love Texas history because it's the tale of our ancestors' lives. For centuries, our mothers and fathers were born and died on this soil, and we must honor them. If no one will put on the armor and fight the fight like they did, who will?"

15   No one ever knew that I smuggled food to Ms. De Zavala, using "some cord that showed up one night." My father wasn't too happy about that, of course. After three consecutive days of self-imprisonment, the governor of Texas agreed to preserve the Alamo, and Ms. De Zavala abandoned her post. I couldn't help but feel I had helped fight the fight for Texas's history, too.

1 The author includes imagery of fighting in the Texas Revolution in paragraph 9 to —

A describe how afraid of the rats De Zavala was

B compare De Zavala's imprisonment to other prisons

C explain how De Zavala felt about preserving Texas history

D inform the readers about what happened at the Alamo

2 The dialogue that tells how Ms. De Zavala feels about the Alamo is —

F "I would be telling a falsehood if I said my accommodations were comfortable."

G "If this is what it takes to protect this place, then I'll stay forever if needs be."

H "How can we get the sandwiches all the way up here, though?"

J "Criminals fare better in the town jail with beds and food."

3 Based on the text, what can readers infer about Tim?

A He is worried about getting in trouble for going to the Alamo.

B He wonders what kind of condition the Alamo is in.

C He admires Ms. De Zavala for protecting the Alamo.

D He thinks law enforcement is right to deny her food.

4 What is the theme of the selection?

F Heroism often involves fighting for what you believe.

G Kindness often leads to friendship with new people.

H Patriotism means breaking the law to support your cause.

J Friendship is more important than family.

Quick Tip

When authors use a first-person point of view, the character telling the story lets the reader know how he or she thinks and feels. *Who is the person telling the story? How does he feel about Ms. De Zavala?*

COMPARE AND CONTRAST THEMES

- In the **Literature Anthology,** reread the poems "Birdfoot's Grandpa" on page 501 and "Growing Up" on page 504.

- Use the Venn diagram to show what is the same and what is different about the themes.

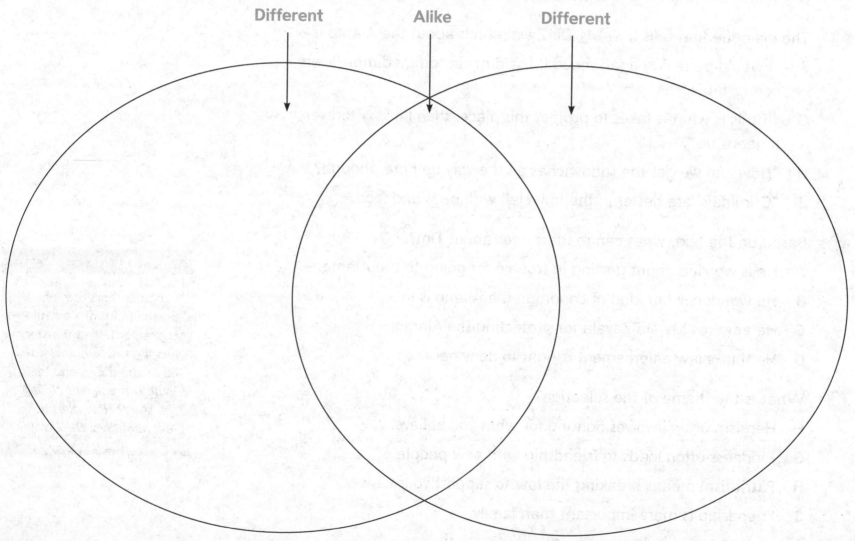

Different   Alike   Different

VOICE

Voice shows how a writer thinks and feels about a topic. A poet chooses a voice (or multiple voices) for a poem to engage the reader's attention. The language or words that the poet chooses help shape the voice and can make it happy, sad, energetic, or moody.

Reread the poem "the drum" by Nikki Giovanni on page 500 of the **Literature Anthology.** Then answer the questions below.

- Who is the speaker of the poem? _____.

- What point of view did the poet use in the poem? _____.

- What can you tell about the speaker from her voice? Use text evidence.

  _____

  _____

PERSONIFICATION

Personification is a type of figurative language that gives animals, ideas, and objects human qualities. For example, *Trees waved in the wind* means trees were moving in a certain way. With a partner, review the nouns below. Write a sentence for each word, using personification to make each sentence interesting.

ants _____

cactus _____

wind _____

WRITE HISTORICAL FICTION

Historical fiction is a story that is written about real events, people, or places. Research an important historical event that happened in your state in the nineteenth century. Write a short historical fiction piece about the event. Include dialogue that someone may have said. Think about how the historical and cultural setting will impact the plot. Use the graphic organizer below to plan the sequence of events in your story.

I chose this event in my state's history because _____

_____.

> **Beginning**

> **Middle**

> **End**

CHARGE

Online articles have text features similar to print articles. Online articles also may have interactive elements, such as videos, animations, and links to additional information. Log on to **my.mheducation.com** and read the online *Time For Kids* article "Charge." Pay attention to the information found in the interactive elements. Then, answer the questions below.

Charge!
Electric cars are hitting the road. Will you drive one someday?

Time For Kids: "Charge"

- How is a traditional gasoline-powered car different from an electric car? Use information from the article and the linked Diagram of a Hybrid Car.

_____

_____

- Why is it important that Americans "kick the oil habit"?

_____

_____

- What roadblocks remain in the development of oil-free cars?

_____

_____

- Why do carmakers want to make lighter cars?

_____

_____

Yaacov Dagan/Alamy Stock Photo

TRACK YOUR PROGRESS

WHAT DID YOU LEARN?

Use the rubric to evaluate yourself on the skills that you learned in this unit. Write your scores in the boxes below.

4	3	2	1
I can successfully identify all examples of this skill.	I can identify most examples of this skill.	I can identify a few examples of this skill.	I need to work on this skill more.

☐ Theme   ☐ Main Idea and Key Details   ☐ Imagery

☐ Sidebars   ☐ Dialogue   ☐ Make Inferences

☐ Greek Prefixes

Something that I need to work more on is _____ because

_____

_____

_____

Text to Self Think back over the texts that you have read in this unit. Choose one text and write a short paragraph explaining a personal connection that you have made to the text.

I made a personal connection to _____ because _____

_____

_____

_____

Conduct Your Interview

COLLABORATE

Prepare to conduct an interview with a member of your family or a friend's family. Ask about traits that members of the person's family inherited or learned. Use the checklist as you prepare the interview.

An interesting fact that I learned about the person is _____

_____

_____

_____

I would like to know more about _____

_____

_____

_____

Quick Tip

It can be challenging to take notes while someone is talking. Consider recording the interview and taking notes when you listen to the recording later.

✓ **Interview Checklist**

☐ Be prepared. Learn as much about the person as you can.

☐ Write your questions before the interview.

☐ Speak slowly when asking questions.

☐ Listen attentively to the responses.

☐ Take notes and ask for permission to record the interview.

Jeff Greenough/Blend Images/Getty Images